# Mediation Practice Guide

## A HANDBOOK FOR RESOLVING BUSINESS DISPUTES

### Second Edition
*Revised and Expanded*

### Bennett G. Picker

**Defending Liberty
Pursuing Justice**

**American Bar Association
Section of Dispute Resolution**

# MEDIATION PRACTICE GUIDE:
## A Handbook for Resolving Business Disputes
### *Second Edition*

**Published by the American Bar Association Section of Dispute Resolution**
740 15th St. NW, Washington, DC 20005
(202) 662-1680; Fax (202) 662-1683
dispute@abanet.org; www.abanet.org/dispute

| | |
|---|---|
| **Staff Editors:** | **Jack C. Hanna** |
| | **Gina Viola Brown** |
| **Managing Editor:** | **H. Kyo Suh** |
| **Cover Art:** | **Lisa Benn** |

The materials contained herein represent the opinions of the author(s) and should not be construed to be the action of either the American Bar Association or the Section of Dispute Resolution, unless adopted pursuant to the bylaws of the Association.

Nothing contained in this book is to be considered as the rendering of legal advice for specific cases, and readers are responsible for obtaining such advice from their own legal counsel. This book and any forms and agreements herein are intended for educational and informational purposes only.

ISBN: 1-59031-169-8

Discounts are available for members of the ABA Section of Dispute Resolution and for books ordered in bulk. Special consideration is given to state bars, CLE programs, other bar-related organizations and educational institutions. For book orders, inquire at the American Bar Association Service Center, 750 North Lake Shore Drive, Chicago, Illinois 60611. (312) 988-5522. Or contact the Section of Dispute Resolution, (202) 662-1680.

# TABLE OF CONTENTS

## CHAPTER 1
## MEDIATION AND THE LANDSCAPE OF ADR

## CHAPTER 2
## THE DECISION TO MEDIATE

## CHAPTER 3
## THE STAGES OF A TYPICAL MEDIATION

## CHAPTER 4
## THE ROLE OF THE MEDIATOR

# CHAPTER 5
# NEGOTIATION AND MEDIATION –
# OVERCOMING THE BARRIERS TO RESOLUTION

# CHAPTER 6
# PREPARING FOR MEDIATION

## CHAPTER 7
## REPRESENTING THE CLIENT IN THE MEDIATION

## CHAPTER 8
## CASE STUDIES IN MEDIATION

## CHAPTER 9
## CORPORATE AND LAW FIRM
## ADR STRATEGIES

## CHAPTER 10
## THE FUTURE OF MEDIATION – NEW CHALLENGES AND OPPORTUNITIES FOR THE LEGAL PROFESSION

# APPENDICES

# PREFACE

This book is intended to serve as a practical guide—a primer—to assist lawyers and parties in navigating the landscape of mediation.

Mediation has become a powerful tool to resolve business and other disputes early, cost-effectively and fairly. Of course, mediation should not be thought of as a substitute for litigation. Indeed, there is no substitute for strong trial skills and good case preparation. However, in the appropriate case, mediation can create a more direct, less risky and less costly path toward a favorable resolution. A skilled mediator can work with parties to a dispute to facilitate communication and to explore the potential for business-driven solutions. Many of these solutions are simply unavailable in the "win-lose" environment of litigation.

My own practice has moved substantially into the world of mediation and conflict management over the past fifteen years. As a mediator, I am continually reminded that mediation often represents unfamiliar terrain to even the most experienced litigator and transactional lawyer. This practical guide is intended to serve as a resource for lawyers and business persons who are considering mediation or preparing for the process.

I have attempted to make this book "user friendly," keeping it fairly simple and providing checklists wherever possible. I also have concentrated on the key mediation issues—suitability, preparation and advocacy. Since the book is a primer, I have not addressed more complex issues such as cultural issues in cross-border disputes or the consequences of mediation where there is an imbalance of power. Nor have I given thorough treatment to such issues as negotiating theory or mediator style. For a more exhaustive study of these and other important topics, I refer the reader to "Suggested Readings" in the Appendix.

Our society is currently undergoing a dramatic change in the culture of dispute resolution. In recent years, those of us on the front line of dispute resolution can almost feel the velocity of change in attitudes toward resolving disputes. Courts, government agencies and clients increasingly have demanded consideration of alternative options, especially the alternative of mediation in business disputes. Law firms are beginning to respond to the challenges and opportunities presented by these demands. As we begin the 21st century, litigators and transactional lawyers need to have a better understanding of mediation to serve the interests of their clients properly. My own view is that consideration of mediation and other ADR options is, simply stated, responsible lawyering.

Lawyers who are familiar with the landscape of mediation and are well prepared for the process will have significant opportunities to add value to their clients. It is my hope that this practice guide will contribute meaningfully to those efforts.

# ABOUT THE AUTHOR

Bennett G. Picker is a senior partner in the Philadelphia law firm of Stradley Ronon Stevens & Young, LLP, where he concentrates his law practice in the area of alternative dispute resolution. He chairs the firm's ADR Practice Group.

Mr. Picker has an active ADR practice, serving both as a mediator and arbitrator in business disputes and as an advocate in negotiations and mediations on behalf of clients. He is a member of the Panel of Distinguished Neutrals and the Employment Panel of the CPR Institute for Dispute Resolution, a member of the Commercial Mediation and Arbitration Panels of the American Arbitration Association, a member of the Mediation Panels of the Court of Arbitration for Sport (Lausanne, Switzerland) and World Intellectual Property Organization (Geneva, Switzerland) and a Certified Mediator, United States District Court for the Eastern District of Pennsylvania.

Mr. Picker is a Fellow of the American College of Civil Trial Mediators and a Fellow of the International Academy of Mediators. He also serves as a member of the Board of Directors of the American Arbitration Association and has served as Co-Chair of the Association's National Mediation Committee.

Mr. Picker has written extensively and lectured widely on the subject of mediation. He has authored numerous articles on mediation and negotiation and co-authored (with Jack Foltz) the chapter on "ADR" in a multi-volume series entitled *Successful Partnering Between Inside and Outside Counsel* (West Group and American Corporate Counsel Association, 2000). In addition, he has been a lecturer or trainer in programs sponsored by the American and Pennsylvania Bar Associations, Practicing Law Institute, Centre for Effective Dispute Resolution (United Kingdom), CPR Institute for Dispute Resolution, American Arbitration Association, American Corporate Counsel Association and numerous law schools and in-house legal departments of corporations throughout the United States.

An active participant in the Philadelphia Bar Association, Mr. Picker served as the Bar Association's Chancellor and as Chairman of the Bar Association's Board of Governors, Judiciary Committee and Appellate Courts Committee. He is a founder and Advisory Board member of Pennsylvanians for Modern Courts, a former member of the Pennsylvania Trial Court Nominating Commission (First Judicial District), a founding board member of Meritas (an international affiliation of law firms) and a member of the Advisory Board of Hildebrandt, Inc.

Mr. Picker is a graduate, *magna cum laude*, of Temple University and the Columbia University School of Law where he served as Executive Editor of the *Columbia Journal of Transnational Law*.

# CHAPTER 1

## MEDIATION AND THE LANDSCAPE OF ADR

## §1.1    INTRODUCTION

*A story often told to illustrate the advantages of mediation involves two children fighting over the last orange remaining in the refrigerator. The parent, overhearing the argument, and with Solomon-like wisdom, resolved the dispute by telling the children to share the orange equally by splitting the orange in half. In contrast, a mediator would have asked both of the children "Why do you want the orange?" Upon hearing that one child wanted to make orange juice and the other wanted to make marmalade, a mediator would have facilitated a better result by encouraging one child to take the juice of the whole orange and the other to take the rind and pulp. This example illustrates how mediation offers the potential for "win-win" solutions.* See *Fisher, Roger and William Ury*, Getting To Yes: Negotiating Agreement Without Giving In *(Houghton Mifflin Co. 1981).*

More than a decade ago, a leading national advocate of alternative dispute resolution (ADR) referred to mediation as the "sleeping giant of ADR." In only a decade, we have seen this giant awake – parties are now commonly providing for mediation in dispute resolution provisions in contracts and voluntarily turning to the process when disputes arise. Although arbitration clearly has a significant and appropriate role in dispute resolution, it often suffers from the same limitations as litigation—it is rights-based and can be as costly and time-consuming as litigation. As a consequence, not only are parties increasingly turning to voluntary mediation as a means of resolving business disputes, but court systems and governmental agencies are also mandating mediation and some states are amending rules of professional conduct to require the consideration of ADR and mediation. In the appropriate case, lawyers and clients are finding mediation to be *the* most powerful tool to resolve business disputes early, cost effectively and fairly.

Mediation has dramatically changed the landscape of dispute resolution in our society. As a consequence, in virtually every case, lawyers (and parties to disputes) need to determine whether a dispute should be resolved by negotiation, litigation, mediation, or some other form of ADR. To provide clients with the benefit of ADR counseling and advocacy at sophisticated levels, lawyers engaged in dispute resolution and litigation need to become fully acquainted with the process of mediation.

## §1.2    MEDIATION DEFINED

Mediation is a process that employs a neutral person—the mediator—to facilitate negotiations between parties to a dispute in an effort to reach a mutually acceptable resolution. Mediations are:

- voluntary

- flexible

- confidential

- informal

- non-binding

Unlike an arbitrator or a judge, a mediator does not impose a solution on the parties to a dispute. Instead, a mediator works with the parties to assist them in defining their objectives and achieving a resolution of their differences. Although mediation is a non-binding process, the result of this process in the vast majority of cases is an agreement that is both binding and enforceable.

Mediation often redefines the way in which parties view a dispute by looking beyond positional bargaining over issues such as who "breached" and the extent of a party's "damages." The process creates an opportunity to explore underlying business interests and to examine the relationships between parties to a dispute. A skilled mediator, therefore, can help the parties overcome hostilities and legal posturing and can often develop creative, business-driven solutions. For example, claims for breaches of distributorship agreements have been settled by redefining territorial limits. Claims for breaches of agreements between vendor and vendee have been settled by agreements on future price discounts. In disputes between partners or shareholders who are also members of the same family, apologies have served as the linchpin of settlements. As these examples demonstrate, mediation offers the potential for a "win-win" solution in contrast to arbitration and litigation where there is a winner and a loser.

Even in a "pure dollars" dispute, a mediator can facilitate communications, assist the parties in making a realistic assessment of their case and help structure creative means of monetary exchange.

## §1.3    MEDIATION AS FACILITATED NEGOTIATION

Parties often experience frustration and difficulty in settlement negotiations. In addition to the inherent problems arising from the fact that the parties in a negotiation have opposing views and conflicting goals, other issues, such as personal antagonisms, make the process of communication difficult. Involving a mediator usually changes the dynamics of a negotiation.

A skilled mediator can enhance the process of communication and negotiation by working with the parties to:

- provide focus

- manage the agenda

- clarify misunderstandings

- reduce tension

- frame issues

- explore new areas of discussion

- help parties make realistic assessments

- set the pace of negotiations

- coach the parties on moves in negotiations

- make suggestions for mutually acceptable solutions

- ensure fairness in the process

A mediator typically accomplishes these objectives by meeting with all parties and their counsel, in joint meetings and in separate caucuses, as may be appropriate. In contrast to direct negotiations between the parties or even litigation settlement conferences, a mediator usually will insist upon the presence of those representatives of the parties with ultimate decision-making authority. The mediator will involve these representatives directly in the process of communication and negotiation.

# §1.4 MEDIATION AND ADJUDICATION COMPARED

It is important to understand the distinctions between the characteristics of mediation and those of adjudicative forums (arbitration and litigation). The following chart summarizes the major differences:

| MEDIATION | ADJUDICATION |
|---|---|
| • parties retain control over outcome | • parties relinquish control to third party |
| • neutral assists parties in defining issues and exploring interests and possible resolutions | • arbitrator/judge listens to evidence and renders decision |
| • potential for compromise is determined by the parties | • little potential for compromise — decisions made based upon facts and law |
| • negotiation is facilitated | • outcome is determined |
| • need for discovery is often minimal | • discovery is often extensive |
| • process is private and confidential | • arbitrations are private (but decisions often available); court hearings and trials are public |
| • parties are encouraged to communicate with each other directly | • all communications are through lawyer to tribunal |

| MEDIATION | ADJUDICATION |
|---|---|
| • focus is on all logically relevant factors including issues, interests, emotions, goals and relationships | • focus is narrow and limited by defined set of rules and procedures |
| • joint and individual caucus meetings are informal | • hearings are formal and evidentiary |
| • outcome is based upon perceptions and needs of parties | • decisions are based upon evidence and law |
| • parties often agree to mutually satisfactory resolution of dispute | • result makes one party a winner, the other a loser |
| • issues in complex dispute can be telescoped in hours or days | • often takes months or years to resolve complex dispute |
| • participants have flexibility to determine ground rules | • participants have little or no flexibility—process governed by one set of rules for all parties |
| • process is low risk and cost-effective | • arbitration costs are usually higher and litigation costs are significantly higher |

## §1.5 MEDIATION AND ALTERNATIVE DISPUTE RESOLUTION (ADR)

It is regrettable that the phrase "alternative dispute resolution" has come to define the growing movement in favor of alternative options. Almost necessarily, the phrase suggests that disputes should be resolved by an "alternative" to litigation. "Appropriate dispute resolution" or "active dispute resolution" more properly would describe a dispute resolution culture that recognizes the need to consider the client's objectives in every case and to develop a strategy designed to accomplish those objectives. Whatever the phrase used to describe the alternatives, it is important to consider all of the options in every case, including negotiation, litigation, arbitration, mediation and other non-traditional options. Moreover, these alternatives should not be regarded as mutually exclusive. In some circumstances, for example, a focused litigation strategy can promote a favorable outcome in mediation and provide a forum in the event a mediation is unsuccessful.

Mediation and binding arbitration are clearly the two leading approaches to resolving disputes out of court. However, there are a number of non-traditional approaches that encompass many of the same features presented by mediation, especially privacy, confidentiality and the opportunity for prompt resolution. Among these approaches are the following:

- mediation-arbitration (med-arb)

- non-binding arbitration

- bounded arbitration

- baseball arbitration

- confidential listening

- early neutral evaluation

- minitrial

- multi-party coordinated defense

- ombuds

- partnering

In the next several years, we are likely to see a proliferation of hybrid uses of mediation, binding arbitration and the more non-traditional approaches as parties to disputes increasingly turn to non-traditional dispute resolution options.

# §1.6    MEDIATION—ARBITRATION (MED-ARB)

In a med-arb proceeding, parties agree in advance that any issues unresolved in mediation will be resolved in binding arbitration by a neutral serving in the dual role of mediator and arbitrator. Parties opting for a single neutral to perform both roles often do so in an effort to save costs. While the prospective role of arbitrator gives the mediator considerable clout, significant advantages may be lost because parties are less likely to be candid with the mediator. For this reason, many mediators will not serve in the dual role of "mediator" and "arbitrator." At the conclusion of a mediation, however, mediators often are willing to serve as an arbitrator to decide minor unresolved issues or issues arising in connection with future related disputes.

When parties agree, by contract or otherwise, to mediation followed by binding arbitration using separate neutrals, this two-step procedure does not present the same problems as a med-arb proceeding. While this two-step procedure is more costly (if the mediation is unsuccessful), the parties are likely to be far more open with the mediator and the chances of success in mediation will be far greater.

Although even the most experienced litigators ask about "binding mediation," there is no such process. The phrase is confusing, for it suggests that the parties can be forced to accept an externally imposed resolution of their dispute. It is the voluntarily participatory nature of mediation that creates the bright line distinguishing "mediation" from "arbitration." Similarly, it would be inappropriate to use the phrase "binding mediation" to refer to a binding commitment to mediate arising from an obligation created by contract or by the court. Of course, a successful mediation can result in a legally binding settlement agreement.

## §1.7    DISPUTE RESOLUTION CLAUSES IN CONTRACTS

Parties to written agreements are paying greater attention to dispute resolution clauses in contracts. Traditionally, it has been common for lawyers to insert an "arbitration clause" in a contract where parties to an agreement prefer arbitration to litigation. However, parties to written agreements are giving greater consideration to various ADR options, and are increasingly insisting on progressive, multi-step contract clauses that require, for example, executive negotiations followed by mediation followed by arbitration (*See* Appendix I).

In some circumstances, parties to a written agreement may prefer mediation as a predicate to the trigger of litigation. In other circumstances, especially where a party anticipates a large volume of small dollar disputes, where the paramount interest is minimizing legal and transactional costs, or in a cross-border transaction, a party may prefer mediation followed by arbitration. *(See § 2.2 Suitability of Dispute for Mediation, for a more detailed explanation of factors favoring and weighing against mediation).* In drafting a dispute resolution clause that provides for arbitration, it is important to focus upon key issues such as the scope of the agreement to arbitrate, the decision to appoint one or three arbitrators, whether or not party-designated arbitrators are neutral or partisan, the tolling of the statute of limitations, the need for a carve-out for injunctive relief, the desire for a bare or reasoned award and the desire to preclude an award for punitive damages.

## §1.8.    EMPLOYMENT ADR

In recent years, an increasing focus on ADR options has resulted in greater attention to the design of systems intended to avoid disputes. For example, the rapidly growing field of "employment ADR" offers companies multi-step ADR programs. These programs typically offer systems designed to permit employees to air their grievances at the earliest possible time so that problems can be resolved before they become full-blown disputes. Specifically, many companies have adopted internal mechanisms for resolving employment conflicts, including the use of ombudspersons, employee hotlines, peer review and progressive management review. Problems not resolved internally are then submitted to mediation followed by arbitration. The Halliburton Dispute Resolution Program, (formerly the Brown & Root Employment ADR Program) has enjoyed great success and has served as a prototype for numerous employment ADR programs implemented by other companies in the past several years (*See* Appendix J). In designing an employment ADR program, it is important to consider issues of corporate culture and the current legal status of agreements to arbitrate employment disputes.

## §1.9    COURT-ANNEXED MEDIATION

In addition to voluntary mediation, many state and federal jurisdictions require mediation of some or all cases filed with the court.

Court-annexed mediation (also known as "court-mandated mediation"), by definition, is not voluntary and lacks some aspects which make voluntary mediation an attractive dispute resolution alternative. For example, the parties do not retain control over procedures and are not free to design the ground rules of the mediation. Further, the process itself is often more like a judicial settlement conference in which the "mediator" is being substituted for the judge. Mediators in this abbreviated format often cannot devote the time necessary to the process of facilitating communication between the parties. In addition, since the parties may not be directly involved in court-annexed mediations, there is less potential in business disputes to develop solutions based upon the parties' underlying interests.

Notwithstanding their limitations, court-annexed programs are achieving some measure of success. By requiring opposing counsel to meet and discuss settlement in the presence of a mediator, court-annexed programs do increase the likelihood of settlement earlier in the litigation. Even though the ground rules of court-annexed programs are more restrictive than those of voluntary mediations, they nonetheless offer opportunities for the neutral to enhance the level of communication between the parties and to act as an agent of reality.

The above observations are made with respect to court programs that require most or all of the cases in the system to be mediated. They are not directed to an instance in which a judge takes a single case out of the system and orders the parties to proceed to mediation. Typically, this latter type of court-ordered mediation has most of the same characteristics as a voluntary mediation.

## §1.10   MEDIATION IN COMPLEX LITIGATION: COOPERATIVE CASE MANAGEMENT

Mediation is most often thought of as an alternative to litigation. However, we are beginning to see an innovative form of mediation *within* the framework of litigation. Multi-party and complex cases and, especially mass disaster cases, offer opportunities for this new form of mediation—the mediation of differences among and between parties in litigation. In many such cases, cooperation in the initial stages of litigation is difficult as many defendants seek to minimize their own exposure and to maximize the responsibility and exposure of co-defendants. In complex cases involving multiple defendants, the pursuit of cross-claims and the inability to cooperate can often be prescriptions for disaster.

Defendants in such cases can achieve significant benefits by jointly retaining a mediator (or facilitator) to work with all defendants toward common goals such as (1) entering into a joint or cooperative defense agreement; (2) removing cross-claims from the court system to an agreed-upon process of alternative dispute resolution; and (3) coordinating cooperation in discovery, motion practice and preparation for trial.

In recent years, in cooperation with the CPR Institute for Dispute Resolution, a mediator was able to achieve some or all of these benefits on behalf of the more than 40 "product and service" defendants in the *One Meridian Plaza Fire Litigation* in Philadelphia; on behalf of the product defendants in the *Happy Land Social Club* litigation in New York; and on behalf of defendants in the *DuPont Plaza* litigation in San Juan, Puerto Rico.

Among the benefits that can be achieved as the result of a cooperative defense agreement are the following:

- informal discovery among and between defendants

- joint efforts to build a defense

- joint fact investigations

- jointly retained experts

- cooperation among experts

- cooperation in formal discovery

- exploration of global settlement possibilities

- savings on transcripts, document management and other costs

A cooperative litigation management strategy must take into account the inherent conflict between target defendants and peripheral defendants. The parties also must address the difficult issues surrounding the desire of a party to control the litigation as well as legal issues involving work product and privilege. With the assistance of a skilled mediator, most of the difficult issues can be resolved to the satisfaction of the participating parties.

Defendants in complex and multi-party cases can achieve important strategic advantages and significant savings through cooperation and the use of a mediator. In coming years, we are likely to see this innovative form of mediation used with increasing frequency.

# CHAPTER 2

## THE DECISION TO MEDIATE

## §2.1    INTRODUCTION

The decision to mediate is often driven by the general advantages of mediation discussed in the preceding chapter. When drafting a dispute resolution clause in a written agreement, counsel should examine whether mediation is likely to advance the client's interests given the kinds of disputes most likely to arise (*See* §1.7 Dispute Resolution Clauses in Contracts). In the absence of a written agreement, each particular dispute must be examined by each party on its own merits to determine whether mediation is the best alternative. This chapter discusses the key issues in making the decision to mediate—whether to mediate, when to mediate, why mediation succeeds or fails, and how to propose mediation.

## §2.2    SUITABILITY OF DISPUTE FOR MEDIATION

### §2.2.1    Introduction

In every dispute, counsel should consider whether a client's objectives can best be achieved through negotiation, litigation, mediation or some other form of alternative dispute resolution. While mediation is not "one size fits all," the benefits and disadvantages of mediation should be discussed with the client in virtually every business dispute.

Not every case is appropriate for mediation. In some cases, mediation is not necessary to achieve a negotiated resolution. Parties often overlook the possibility of resolving a dispute through direct and unassisted negotiations—an option that should be examined in every case. (*See* Chapter 5 Negotiation and Mediation – Overcoming the Barriers to Resolution). In other cases, litigation may be the best dispute resolution alternative. For example, in a product liability case in which a plaintiff seeks to develop a new theory of liability, a defendant may decide that the need to establish a precedent dictates that litigation is the best alternative. Similarly, litigation may be the best alternative if a party needs injunctive relief or is defending a frivolous lawsuit.

Most cases that are suitable for a negotiated resolution are also suitable for mediation. This is particularly true if client participation is needed to resolve the dispute. Moreover, a dispute may be ripe for mediation notwithstanding the fact that there have been failed negotiations in the past or the fact that the controversy is the subject of a pending lawsuit.

### §2.2.2    Factors Favoring Mediation

Some disputes are particularly suitable for mediation. Factors favoring mediation include:

- need to avoid publicity/need for confidentiality or privacy

- desire for speedy resolution/need to avoid delay

- need to preserve continuing relationship

- recognition that emotions or hostilities may bar a settlement

- desire to minimize risk of an imposed outcome

- need to reduce high costs of litigation

- no adequate remedy at law

- desire to avoid adverse precedent

- no need to establish a precedent

- existence of collateral issues that may enhance resolution in a mediation forum

### §2.2.3     Factors Weighing Against Mediation

The nature of some disputes suggests litigation as the most appropriate dispute resolution alternative. Factors weighing against mediation include:

- need to establish a legal precedent

- absence of a bona fide dispute—other side's case is frivolous

- entire case likely to be decided on motion to dismiss or motion for summary judgment

- need for time to elapse before settlement possibilities can be evaluated

- other parties are not yet aware of dispute or have not yet been identified and need to be included for proper resolution of the dispute

- authorized decision maker is not available

- current budget limitations prevent serious settlement negotiations

- settlement was reached in the past, but a party breached the settlement agreement

- parties do not want a settlement

- need for immediate equitable relief

In deciding whether to mediate, parties should also consider the factors which may suggest binding arbitration as the best dispute resolution alternative. These include, among others, the need for prompt resolution, the desire for privacy, the need to minimize litigation costs, the existence of bad faith in prior negotiations, the high probability that a negotiated settlement is unlikely even in a mediation setting and the absence of any compelling reason to seek relief in a court of law.

### §2.2.4      Suitability Screening

The CPR Institute for Dispute Resolution developed a "suitability screen" to assist in making the determination of whether a case is appropriate for mediation or some other non-traditional dispute resolution alternative. Some law firms and corporations have also developed their own suitability screens (*See* Appendix C). These screens allow for a more sophisticated analysis than the list of factors provided in the preceding section. Further, many corporations have adopted formal procedures to institutionalize the analysis of suitability issues. For example, some corporations have a designated ADR counsel to monitor all disputes for this purpose. In addition, some corporations require their outside law firms to justify in writing why a dispute is inappropriate for ADR before allowing a dispute to proceed in the normal course (*See* §9.2 Corporate ADR Strategies).

## §2.3      TYPES OF BUSINESS DISPUTES COMMONLY MEDIATED

Virtually all types of business disputes which are appropriate and ripe for negotiated resolution can be mediated. Certain types of business disputes have factors which make the dispute particularly suitable for mediation. For example, construction disputes require real time solutions to avoid project delays. Contract disputes involving continuing relationships between parties can often be resolved by restructuring relationships. Many employment disputes also afford an opportunity to preserve the relationship between employer and employee. In some instances, mediation not only offers a process to resolve existing disputes but also promotes better lines of communication which tend to reduce future problems.

Business disputes that are commonly mediated with success include:

-      bankruptcy and creditor/debtor

- commercial, financial and real estate transactions

- claims against professionals

- construction

- franchise

- employment

- environmental

- insurance coverage

- intellectual property/technology

- partnership

- product liability

- regulatory matters

- securities

- trademark and unfair competition

## §2.4    DECIDING WHEN TO MEDIATE

While every dispute has its own time-related constraints and imperatives, it is generally advisable to mediate a dispute sooner rather than later. Of course, a mediation too early in the life of a dispute may be unproductive. The parties may need time to obtain the information necessary for a more meaningful evaluation of the merits of a case. At the same time, parties to disputes routinely resolve their differences through direct, unassisted negotiations without having made a comprehensive investigation of the facts and legal positions. Moreover, even where additional information is necessary in order to make a reasonable evaluation, a mediator can assist the parties in reaching agreements concerning the exchange of information. When the parties' efforts to achieve a negotiated resolution fail, mediation should be considered as a possible next step. At this juncture, parties are often still flexible in their positions and are usually interested in the cost savings that will result from avoiding litigation.

In some cases, mediation may be unproductive too early in a dispute because hostilities prevent the parties from communicating effectively. Mediation also may be unproductive because a party, convinced of the correctness of its position, is not prepared to consider an early compromise—a barrier to settlement that is often removed once a party incurs substantial costs in litigation. If parties to a dispute wait too long before considering mediation, however, the parties may become too committed to their positions to consider any solution other than litigation.

## §2.5    WHY MEDIATION WORKS

Most mediations of business disputes are successful because of the following reasons:

- *Greater efficiency*. Mediation is a more efficient way of resolving most disputes. Parties can often telescope in days or hours the facts and legal issues likely to take months or years to develop in litigation. As a consequence, parties can avoid substantial costs in legal fees, litigation expense, and indirect costs associated with a protracted legal action.

- *Interest-based solutions*. As the mediator identifies and explores underlying interests and concerns beyond the legal issues and dollar amounts in a dispute, the parties can "enlarge the pie" before dividing it. Parties have the opportunity and incentive to formulate business-driven solutions not available either in court or in arbitration.

- *Barriers to resolution identified*. Mediation offers an opportunity to identify and overcome potential barriers to a negotiated resolution, such as differing perceptions, party problems, issue problems and extrinsic pressures (*See* § 5.2 The Common Barriers to Resolution).

- *More effective communication*. Mediation gives the parties the opportunity to communicate more effectively and to discover common ground through interest-based exploration or other means. In a mediation setting, the parties have an opportunity to speak out on any issue or concern without regard to legal relevance. In a process which is very personal, parties develop a sense of investment in the outcome and are more open to changing their perceptions about a dispute when they listen to the other side.

- *Control by parties*. Participants in mediation have control of not only the outcome but also the process. The process is flexible and can be designed in the manner best suited to achieve a client's goals and objectives (e.g., limited discovery or no discovery, with or without written submissions, with controlled exchanges by experts where advisable).

- *Privacy and confidentiality*. The private and confidential nature of the process allows for more open communications than in arbitration or litigation (*See* §6.9 Protect Confidentiality) which enhances the possibility of settlement. Parties are less reluctant to disclose sensitive information once they become comfortable with the mediator and the mediation environment. Many businesses opt for mediation to avoid adverse publicity which may have an even larger negative impact upon the company than the dispute itself.

- *Foundation for later resolution*. Even when a dispute is not resolved in the formal mediation process, a foundation is often set for a later resolution either directly by the parties or with the mediator's continued involvement.

## §2.6    WHY SOME MEDIATIONS FAIL

A failed mediation is often more a result of the participants' lack of understanding of the process than any failure of the process itself. Lawyers often do not understand mediation or are not prepared for the process. Some are even unaware of the fundamental differences between arbitration and mediation.

The relatively unstructured nature of the mediation process makes certain lawyers uncomfortable. They are far more accustomed to litigation and the boundaries dictated by rules of evidence and procedure. Some lawyers do not understand, for example, that the client will be directly involved in the process or will be asked questions such as "what do you need the most" or "how do you feel" about the adverse party. While these questions may be completely unrelated to the merits of the claims and defenses in a lawsuit, they reveal perceptions and interests which affect the process and promote opportunities for resolution.

Other lawyers believe, incorrectly, that there is no downside in a mediation since the process is non-binding and they do little preparation. As a result, significant opportunities to achieve client objectives are often lost by such counsel.

Some mediations fail because of a communications failure, not between the parties or their representatives, but between a lawyer and his or her client. Some lawyers give their clients unrealistic expectations or simply neglect to advise their clients about the merits of their case on a regular basis. In these instances, clients are left without any realistic ability to assess the risks of litigation (*See* Chapter 6 Preparing for Mediation).

Additional reasons why some mediations are unsuccessful include:

- absence of key decision maker

- absence of necessary party

- wrong client representative in the room

- case not suitable for mediation

- mediation occurs before parties have adequate information to make reasonable settlement evaluation

- different and inflexible estimates of litigation risk

- failure to identify or understand the other side's motivations, perspectives and perceptions

- hostilities so great that they prevent the parties from communicating effectively

- lack of patience and perseverance

Finally, some mediations fail because the mediator is either unskilled or inappropriate for the case. In opting for mediation, selecting a *skilled* and *experienced* mediator is the single most important step a party can take to enhance the likelihood of a successful outcome (*See* §6.6 Select the Mediator).

## §2.7    PROPOSING MEDIATION TO AN ADVERSARY

Once the client has opted for mediation, counsel should develop a specific proposal for mediation to present to opposing parties. Besides presenting the generic benefits of mediation, such as speed, cost savings, time savings and privacy, counsel should outline specific benefits likely to serve the opposing party's particular needs.

Assessing the interests of opposing parties will help counsel determine whether the opposing party has an incentive to litigate or mediate. For example, the opposing party may desire a public forum, an interest that will not be served through mediation. Once counsel has assessed the other side's interests, counsel can present a customized proposal that demonstrates to the other side the benefits offered by mediation.

Some lawyers are reluctant to propose mediation because of a concern that the suggestion will be interpreted as a sign of weakness. While the concern should be far less than when making direct overtures to settle, a proposal to mediate can be made in such a manner as to convey a sign of strength. For example, counsel can suggest that the merits of the client's positions are so strong that any skilled mediator would no doubt validate this opinion.

If it is significantly in the client's interest to mediate, counsel should consider including specific incentives for the opposing side if they are reluctant to participate in the process. For example, the party proposing mediation might offer to pay for the initial mediation session. Counsel may also want to consider accepting as the mediator a candidate proposed by the other side so long as the mediator is competent and no conflict exists.

Counsel should also examine the corporate culture of the opposing party. If a party to a dispute has adopted a corporate policy favoring ADR, counsel can remind the party of this commitment made prior to the dispute. More specifically, counsel should determine whether an opposing party is a signator to the CPR Corporate Policy Statement on Alternatives to Litigation. Over 4,000 companies have committed to this pledge which obliges subscribing companies to seriously explore negotiation, mediation or other ADR processes in conflicts arising with other signatories before pursuing full-scale litigation (*See* Appendix B-1). Additionally, many companies have entered into industry-wide "treaties" favoring alternative approaches in disputes between signatory companies.

Some private organizations provide services that will assist in proposing mediation to opposing parties. A neutral person or organization may be in a better position to educate a reluctant party about the benefits of mediation. These organizations are also in a position to provide a range of related services including the submission of mediator candidates and administration of the entire mediation process.

# CHAPTER 3

## THE STAGES OF A TYPICAL MEDIATION

## §3.1    INTRODUCTION

While mediations vary in style, length and rules of conduct, most mediations fall into similar patterns. It is important for parties and counsel in a mediation to understand these patterns in order to maximize the potential for a successful result. The following is a brief discussion of the various stages of a typical mediation.

## §3.2    THE STAGES OF A TYPICAL MEDIATION

### §3.2.1    Preliminary Conference with Mediator—Establishing Ground Rules

After the parties select the mediator (*See* §6.6 Select the Mediator), the mediator usually will start the process by convening a conference of all counsel by telephone or in person to select location, dates and times and to establish the ground rules for the mediation. The mediator will then confer with counsel to get a basic understanding of the controversy and to determine what advance preparation is necessary. If a dispute is in litigation, the mediator will determine what pleadings, memoranda, written expert reports, underlying transactional documents or other writings need to be reviewed in advance of the mediation. In this initial stage, the parties and the mediator will also determine the terms of engagement.

The mediator will discuss with the parties what written statements, if any, should be prepared specifically for the mediation, what oral presentations should be made at the mediation and which representatives of the parties should participate in the mediation.

The following is a list of preliminary matters typically covered in the initial conference with a mediator:

- ground rules and possible modifications

- each party's need for documents or information from the other party

- submission of written statements and other documents to mediator prior to the first session

- appropriate representatives of the parties who will attend the mediation and the extent of their authority

- identification of any non-party stakeholders who should also attend mediation

- scheduling of any *ex parte* conferences prior to the mediation

- scheduling of dates, time and location of mediation sessions

- mediator's terms of engagement

- allocation of mediation fees (especially in multi-party cases)

### §3.2.2    Deciding Who Should Attend Mediation

Before the mediation, the mediator usually will discuss with counsel which representatives of the parties should attend and whether it is necessary to have higher level management representatives, insurance carriers or others present at the mediation. Unless the key decision makers are present, the mediation process will not have its best chance for success. If the representatives require higher levels of authority for final approval of a settlement, the mediator will discuss the need to have these persons available.

If the presence of additional persons is likely to advance the process, the mediator will encourage their participation in the mediation. For example, a mediator may encourage a businessperson who relies on an accountant for business advice to have the accountant present at the mediation.

With respect to issues such as participation, exchange of information and other matters relating to the structure of the mediation, the parties may decide these questions in advance of selecting a mediator in a manner best suited to the controversy. Flexibility in the design of the process is one of the key advantages of mediation. The parties should also recognize that the mediator may have additional insights about structure that will enhance the likelihood of a successful mediation.

### §3.2.3    Limited Exchange of Information

One of the goals of mediation is to avoid costly and time-consuming discovery. While mediations are often held without any agreements on discovery, it may be necessary for the parties to exchange certain materials and documents as a preliminary step to an effective negotiation. For example, a plaintiff will invariably be encouraged to submit to a defendant, in advance of the mediation, a statement supporting its claim for damages. The mediator, therefore, usually will ask the parties whether they need to exchange information or documents in recognition of the fact that gaps in information may cause the mediation to fail.

### §3.2.4 Pre-Mediation Written Submissions and Conferences

While pre-mediation submissions are required in most mediations, the content of these submissions varies greatly. Mediators may require the parties to exchange submissions, especially if the mediation occurs early in the life of a dispute and the parties need to learn more about each other's legal positions.

Either in addition to any exchanged submissions or as the only required submission, most mediators will require a confidential ("eyes-only") submission. In this confidential submission, in addition to a discussion of the parties' respective legal positions, the mediator will ask the parties to discuss the history of any settlement negotiations, any underlying problems in the dispute, any barriers to settlement, any personality issues that need to be considered, corporate policy issues which may be relevant, views concerning underlying interests, and suggestions for creative paths to resolve the dispute.

In substantial or complex disputes, many mediators will hold *ex parte* meetings with counsel and, in some instances, with the parties, in advance of the mediation. In these meetings, the mediator will learn more about the business operations of the parties, obtain necessary confidential information, develop a better understanding of the parties' rights and interests, begin the process of building trust and develop a structure for the mediation best suited to the particular dispute.

## §3.2.5    Initial Joint Session

Most mediations begin with a joint session—representatives of the parties and their counsel assemble together with the mediator in the same room. The session will open with the mediator's introductory remarks which typically will include the following:

- an explanation of the process

- an explanation of the mediator's role in the process

- a statement confirming the mediator's neutrality

- a statement summarizing the mediator's preparation in advance of the proceeding

- a full explanation of the confidential nature of the proceeding

- a statement seeking a commitment from the parties to make a good faith effort to resolve the dispute

In almost all mediations, the parties will have the opportunity to present the highlights of the case in an "opening statement." This opening statement serves a number of purposes. First, it permits each party to argue the strengths of its own position and the weaknesses of positions taken by opposing parties. Second, it affords each party the opportunity to present its case directly to the key decision maker within the adverse party's organization. As a consequence, each party hears the other side's arguments unfiltered by its own counsel. Third, it gives the client representatives an opportunity to tell their story to the other side as well as an opportunity for their "day in court" before moving on to the business of settlement. Fourth, it permits the mediator to be educated further on the issues and to seek clarification by asking follow-up questions.

Given the potentially volatile nature of the process, the mediator usually will exercise a high degree of control at the beginning of the initial joint session. Parties will be permitted, even encouraged, to express their feelings, but they will not be permitted to be overly argumentative. The mediator will prevent the initial session from getting out of control and will intercede if the parties become intransigent or threaten to abandon the mediation process.

At the conclusion of the initial presentations in a joint session, many mediators will ask questions for the purpose of clarifying facts or legal positions. In some instances, a mediator will ask questions (knowing the answers in advance) solely to permit one of the disputants to gain a better understanding of its adversary's positions or perspectives.

## §3.2.6    Initial Caucus Session

Typically, the mediator will separate the parties and meet with them privately at the conclusion of the initial joint conference. In some cases, however, depending on the mediator's own style and especially where the parties in a joint session are engaging in meaningful and constructive dialogue, the mediator will not separate the parties (at least initially).

Separate "caucus" sessions permit the mediator to identify and explore underlying interests and goals and to clarify each party's perspectives. In these sessions, the mediator will encourage the parties to speak more openly and to disclose confidential information in order to identify barriers to settlement and to assist parties in overcoming these barriers (*See* § 5.2 The Common Barriers to Resolution). The mediator will remind the parties of the mediator's obligation not to disclose confidential information. If the mediator believes that disclosure of confidential information will help advance a party's interests, the mediator will seek express authorization to communicate this information to the other side before making any such disclosure.

In most commercial disputes, mediators will move relatively quickly into separate sessions. Typically, parties will feel the need to argue the merits of their positions further at the outset of the initial caucus session. Rarely will the parties open up to a mediator quickly. Instead, they will often try to convince the mediator of the correctness of their positions in an effort to have him or her serve as an advocate in the negotiations (*See* §4.5 The Mediator As Negotiator).

The mediator invariably will anticipate the parties' need to reargue their positions. Given the need to build trust, the mediator will take time to listen to these arguments and will remind the parties that the mediator must remain impartial in order to assist the parties in resolving the dispute. The mediator's patience and articulated confidence in the process is key to a successful mediation.

The mediator will use the early phase of the initial caucus sessions to establish a rapport with the parties, to earn the trust of the parties, to identify the negotiating styles of the attorneys and the identity of the real decision makers and to begin to shift the parties away from their initial positions. In time, the mediator will try to move the parties away from finger pointing and assessing blame to a focus on interests and a problem-solving approach to the dispute.

If, as is often the case, attorneys take the lead in the joint session, the mediator in the caucus session will involve the party representatives by posing questions directly to them. It is not uncommon for a mediator to direct questions to representatives of the parties such as: "How do you assess your own case?" "What are your weaknesses?" "How do you feel about this dispute?" "What do you really want?" "What do you really need?" "What do you need the most?" "What do you think the other side really wants?" These questions permit the mediator to assess the parties' real needs and open the door to possible solutions.

### §3.2.7    Subsequent Joint and Caucus Sessions

After the initial caucus sessions, the hard work of negotiation begins—moving the parties to the common ground of mutual agreement. Typically, the mediator will not issue evaluations or opinions during this process (*See* §4.4 Mediator Styles and Approaches). Rather, the mediator will employ a number of techniques designed to test the limitations of the positions previously taken by the parties (*See* §4.6 Mediator Techniques And Strategies).

In follow-up caucus sessions, the mediator is likely to play "devil's advocate"—testing the validity of positions without revealing his or her own views. The mediator will encourage the parties to consider their risks and costs if the dispute is not resolved at the mediation stage and to assess their alternatives to any proposed negotiated resolution. The mediator will also make an effort to move the parties away from positional bargaining over the strengths and weaknesses of the so-called "merits" and toward the underlying business interests.

Using shuttle diplomacy, the mediator will brainstorm with the parties to identify settlement possibilities and will move between the parties, carrying perspectives and suggesting settlement proposals. This is the most sensitive stage of the communication process. It is imperative that a mediator not communicate to the other side a party's position on settlement without an express understanding that he or she is released to do so. Any breach of this commitment may well lead to a breakdown of the entire proceeding.

In some mediations, the mediator will continue to move between the parties in caucus sessions and will not suggest any further joint session until the end of the process. In other mediations, a return to joint sessions may prove to be helpful, especially where it is necessary to clarify information or where the parties are making an effort to restructure a business relationship.

## §3.2.8    Agreement

When a mediation is successful and the parties reach a settlement, an event which may happen at any point in the process, the mediator will insist that the parties execute a written settlement memorandum or term sheet.

Placing an agreement in writing will reveal whether there is a true "meeting of the minds." Often, a final and comprehensive settlement agreement will follow, one that incorporates all of the terms including general releases from liability. If litigation is pending, parties will agree to terminate the litigation and may also request that the court enter a judgment based on the settlement agreement. The failure to execute a written agreement may well undo all the hard work and may threaten the successful conclusion of the mediation. In the absence of a written agreement, the parties may leave the mediation with differing views as to terms of an agreement or may later have remorse about its terms.

Many mediators discourage the drafting of a full and comprehensive agreement as part of the mediation process. Rather, where such an agreement is necessary, they will encourage the parties to draft the agreement at a later time in order to avoid the potential for a settlement to break down over the drafting process itself. Before closing the proceeding, the mediator will secure agreement from the parties about the drafting and execution of a more comprehensive settlement document. Typically, mediators will offer their continuing assistance with any future problems the parties cannot resolve on their own.

### §3.2.9  Possible Recess, Adjournment and Termination

A mediator will consider a recess for a short period of time in situations where, for example, the parties are not prepared, the parties need more time to reflect upon their settlement positions or additional time is required for higher levels of authorization.

A mediator may adjourn a mediation indefinitely where he or she believes the parties have reached an impasse not likely to be overcome at the mediation session. Recognizing that parties often reassess their positions after a mediation session, the mediator will usually offer to remain available either by telephone or in person for future mediation sessions.

A mediator may determine that an amicable resolution is virtually impossible because there are irreconcilable differences or because one of the parties is unwilling to participate in the manner required. In such a case, the mediator is likely to advise the parties of the problem and terminate the mediation proceeding. However, an experienced mediator will not make such a decision quickly in recognition of the likelihood that obstacles to settlement can be overcome by skillful and patient probing and working through what often appears to the parties to be a hopeless stage in the process.

# CHAPTER 4

## THE ROLE OF THE MEDIATOR

## §4.1    INTRODUCTION

A mediation advocate who understands the perspectives and techniques of the mediator will be in a better position to develop a negotiating strategy designed to accomplish the client's objectives.

It is the presence of an impartial third-party facilitator, the mediator, that distinguishes mediation from traditional negotiation. The mediator's fundamental role is to facilitate communication and compromise among the parties and to help the parties reach an agreement. The mediator neither makes decisions nor judges the fairness of the outcome. Parties decide what is fair, what is not fair, what is acceptable, and what is not acceptable. Thus, it is the parties who are empowered in the mediation process, not the mediator.

## §4.2    QUALITIES OF AN EFFECTIVE MEDIATOR

It is essential that all parties perceive the mediator as a totally impartial facilitator dedicated to working with the parties in an even-handed manner. An effective mediator should have as many of the following qualities as possible:

- absolute impartiality

- trustworthiness

- mediation experience

- good listening skills

- ability to understand the law and facts

- good people skills

- good leadership and management skills

- problem-solving skills

- strong negotiating skills

- flexibility

- good business sense

- patience

- a sense of humor

While all of the above factors are important, it is imperative that a mediator be absolutely impartial, possess strong negotiating skills and have the training and experience to understand the challenges presented by the mediation process. In selecting a mediator, parties also should consider the advantages or disadvantages of substantive expertise, use of facilitative and evaluative styles, and experience as a former judge (*See* §6.6 Select the Mediator).

## §4.3    IMPORTANCE OF CREDIBILITY AND TRUST

For a mediation to have its best chance of success, the mediator must be trustworthy and credible. A mediator can earn the trust of the parties by showing complete impartiality and by actively listening to and reflecting back each party's positions and perspectives. Skilled mediators understand the importance of patience and the need for preparation, professionalism and empathy for the parties' respective positions.

Once a mediator has earned the parties' trust and confidence, the parties to a dispute are likely to be far more open with the mediator and to be more receptive to suggestions and proposals. Conversely, a breach of confidentiality or trust by a mediator will likely result in a failed mediation.

## §4.4 MEDIATOR STYLES AND APPROACHES

Mediators have a variety of different styles and approaches. Generally, styles range from purely facilitative to strongly evaluative. However, there is an ongoing debate in the mediation community concerning the issue of style. Some mediators view mediation as primarily a facilitative process rather than an evaluative one. Some even view "evaluative mediation" as an oxymoron. However, effective mediators generally have flexibility and will use varying degrees of both styles. Moreover, in recent years, many mediators increasingly have recognized that a strong evaluative component is necessary in order to give the process its best chance of success.

The issue of "style" is viewed by mediators in a number of different ways. Some see the dynamics of "facilitative" versus "evaluative" as much a matter of strategy or technique as a matter of style. Some mediators see "style" as a means of distinguishing between interest-based and rights-based approaches, active and passive approaches, or approaches determined by the mediator's personality.

### §4.4.1 Facilitative Style

In using a purely facilitative style, a mediator will assist the parties in identifying and exploring interests, concerns, motivations, goals, common ground and possible resolutions. However, the mediator will avoid drawing conclusions for the parties or offering opinions as to value, legal positions, rights, merits of the case or potential litigation outcomes. In essence, the mediator will not evaluate the case. In facilitative mediation, the parties make all the decisions while the mediator encourages movement through probing and open-ended inquiries.

In pure interest-based facilitative mediation, depending on the subject matter of the dispute, successful resolution does not require the mediator to possess technical or legal expertise. It is usually sufficient for an experienced mediator to be able to understand the dispute and the underlying interests of the parties.

Typically, a facilitative mediator will use caucus sessions to develop the parties' underlying concerns and interests. Spending time alone with the parties is usually necessary to fully explore underlying interests and positions and to identify potential solutions. Joint sessions are often reconvened when parties attempt to resolve a dispute by restructuring old agreements or entering into new ones.

### §4.4.2    Evaluative Style

In using an evaluative style, a mediator is likely to offer opinions on strengths and weaknesses of a case, to challenge the predictions of the parties concerning probable outcomes at trial and to initiate proposals for settlement. Although uncommon, some evaluative mediators first assess the relative merits of the parties' positions and then conduct separate, undisclosed negotiations with each of the parties.

When the participants in a mediation believe that an informed opinion is necessary, a mediator's technical or legal knowledge may help to move negotiations along. Under certain circumstances, a mediator's informed evaluation may assist in breaking an impasse or moving the process toward a final agreement.

A mediator may use an evaluative style when interests are not the primary focus of the parties or when interest-based facilitative mediation is not successful. Since evaluative mediations focus more on the merits of legal positions, the process may bear some resemblance to early neutral evaluation or non-binding arbitration.

Typically, an evaluative mediator will use private caucus sessions to give a party the benefit of an evaluation without disturbing the equilibrium of the negotiations. When a party suggests an evaluation or opinion be given in a joint session to all parties, a mediator will seek the agreement of all parties before issuing such an evaluation or opinion.

An evaluative approach is most often reserved for later stages of the process. Even at this point, however, an evaluative approach is generally used with some degree of caution. When evaluative mediation is being considered, the parties likely will consider whether the mediator is an expert in the subject matter central to the dispute. If evaluative mediation is used, the parties may want the mediator to have knowledge of the "real" facts and all of the applicable law. The mediator also will recognize that comments made in caucus sessions are received without an opportunity for cross-examination or rebuttal.

## §4.4.3    Combined Facilitative and Evaluative Styles

Most disputes require a combination of both facilitative and evaluative styles and approaches. In certain instances, alternating styles may be productive. For example, facilitation may be more effective in building trust and communication in the early stages of mediation, while evaluation may be useful in the later stages in an effort to break an impasse.

Modification of styles may be useful depending on special circumstances of the case and the parties' needs, interests or expectations. For example, a mediator may use a facilitative style to resolve all of the important issues and an evaluative style to assist in the disposition of minor issues.

When asking probing questions or challenging the positions of the participants, usually in caucus sessions, mediators will at times mix facilitative and evaluative styles. These questions or challenges often reflect the mediator's views on important issues, but the practice falls short of a clear statement of the mediator's actual views. By reflecting on such questions, the participants have a greater opportunity to objectively evaluate the strengths and weaknesses of their own positions.

### §4.4.4    Narrow and Broad Approaches

Mediators taking a "narrow" approach are likely to focus on the legal positions taken by the parties. A mediator with a narrow approach will likely proceed with the kind of litigation-risk analysis more typically associated with a judicial settlement conference. In contrast, mediators taking a "broad" approach are likely to move beyond the legal positions taken by the parties to an exploration of the underlying interests. Additionally, a mediator with a broad approach will be more likely to have the parties view a dispute as a "problem" to be solved and, consequently, more likely to have the parties work toward a business solution.

## §4.5    THE MEDIATOR AS NEGOTIATOR

Most mediators perform the multiple roles of confidential listener, facilitator, evaluator and negotiator. As a consequence, there are typically several negotiations proceeding simultaneously, including one between the adverse parties and another between the mediator and each of the parties and their counsel. Given the mediator's agenda, the "negotiations" between the mediator and the parties are usually more cooperative than adversarial.

While the mediator expects some level of cooperation, the parties and counsel are often restrained in their candor because of their need to posture with the mediator. Parties and counsel rarely convey their "bottom line" to the mediator at the outset of a mediation. In time, parties usually become more open to a mediator who has earned their trust in recognition of the fact that partnering with the mediator may create the best opportunity to make progress with the other side (*See* §6.8.10 Develop a Negotiating Plan).

# §4.6    MEDIATOR TECHNIQUES AND STRATEGIES

To be fully prepared for a mediation, counsel should understand the techniques and strategies employed by the mediator. While some mediation techniques are similar to those employed by a judge in a settlement conference, many are specific to the mediation process. Some of the most frequently utilized techniques are discussed below.

## §4.6.1    Information Gathering

In early sessions, the mediator will attempt to gather as much information as possible concerning the parties and the dispute. The mediator will ask open-ended, probing questions to get a sense of the issues and the positions of the parties. The mediator's initial objective will be to identify and explore all the possible elements associated with the contested legal claims including the factual background, the legal issues, the elements of each cause of action, possible defenses, and evidence that supports such claims or defenses.

At this early stage, the mediator will explore the parties' need for settlement, any settlement offer currently on the table, the rationale behind a party's offer, how and why a specific offer was made, what signals such an offer may send to the other side, and why such an offer may be acceptable or unacceptable to the opposing party.

### §4.6.2    Minimizing Hostilities

Especially in caucus sessions, the mediator will allow the parties to express their feelings in an effort to defuse hostility. The mediator's goal is to give the parties a sense that someone is listening to their side without damaging the potential for resolution. By using noninflammatory language and focusing the parties on the key issues, the mediator often can minimize existing hostility. The reduction of hostility may enable each party to better understand the perspective of its adversary and to make a more objective analysis of the dispute.

### §4.6.3    Involving Client Directly

By communicating directly with representatives of the parties, the mediator can overcome the posturing of counsel which typically occurs in a mediation. Parties usually will be more willing than their lawyers to depart from a discussion about legal rights in order to pursue a discussion about underlying concerns and needs. In addition, the mediator will often develop and maintain communication between the parties in an effort to rebuild relationships and to move the parties toward agreement.

### §4.6.4    Prioritizing Client's Concerns and Interests

The mediator usually will help parties identify and rank their concerns, motivations and needs in an attempt to understand fully the parties' underlying interests. During this inquiry, the mediator will direct the focus away from conclusionary positions and will assist the parties in prioritizing their interests and needs. To get to the underlying interests, the mediator may ask non-fact-based questions such as, "How do you feel about this?", "What is most important to you?" and "What is less important?" As the result of such probing, the mediator may uncover interests such as the need to remove an obstacle to a planned merger, the need to avoid being declared in breach of a bank covenant, an interest in avoiding a "hit" on the bottom line in a particular year (or quarter), an interest in avoiding publicity or the desire for an apology. Interests such as these are often as compelling (and sometimes more compelling) than an assessment of the risks and costs of litigation.

### §4.6.5    Active Listening and Paraphrasing

A skilled mediator will listen carefully to representatives of the parties, looking for as many signals as possible from their words and phrases. Words such as "important," "significant," and "substantial" can often convey a sense of the parties' positions on the issues and on possible resolutions. By paraphrasing or summarizing, the mediator can obtain a more complete understanding of the party's positions and avoid the possibility of error when expressing thoughts or positions to the other side. Also, the mediator's paraphrasing helps to clarify for the speaker what he or she is asking. When paraphrasing, the mediator can express thoughts without strong emotional or offensive language. By using these techniques, the mediator also is able to show empathy and enhance the level of trust.

### §4.6.6    Decreasing Commitments to Positions

By probing for underlying interests during the mediation process, the mediator can ease the parties toward interest-based negotiations. In so doing, the focus or commitment to legal rights and positions is relaxed and there is greater opportunity for open communication between the parties. As a result, negotiations become more flexible and new settlement options may be discovered.

### §4.6.7    Focusing Upon Potential to Preserve Relationships

The mediator will focus on the parties' business and strategic interests in reconciling their differences and attempting to reach a settlement. When the potential for a continuing relationship exists, the mediator will explore the advantages of an agreement based upon this relationship. Many disputes can be resolved by restructuring the terms of a relationship and by agreeing on issues such as price discounts, time extensions or the expansion or limitation of territorial rights. Where parties have multiple relationships, some disputes can be resolved by restructuring the terms of a contract which is not the subject of the dispute.

## §4.6.8    Specific Techniques in "Pure Dollars" Disputes

In a "pure dollars" dispute, often referred to as a "distributive" dispute, the ultimate issue between the parties is the division of a sum of money represented by the difference between a demand and an offer. The mediator in such cases invariably will rely heavily on caucus sessions to identify each party's parameters and degree of flexibility. While the mediator will allow the parties to move slowly in order that they may state their case and in an effort to build trust, the mediator will use all of the probing techniques outlined in this chapter to find a way to bridge the gap.

The mediator will often ask the parties to provide a specific justification for their positions on the legal issues and value. However, when the parties are in substantial disagreement on particular issues, the mediator will move away from a discussion about positions to an exploration of the total dollar amount required to reach agreement. The parties are then free to provide their own rationale for any final settlement decisions.

Even in a distributive dispute, the mediator will look for possible creative options such as, for example, the timing of payments. Given the fact that the parties are often unprepared for the fact that a mediation can be a lengthy process, the mediator's principal challenges in orchestrating the negotiations will be to exercise patience, to exhibit optimism and to do what is necessary to keep the parties talking.

## §4.6.9    Reality Testing

By testing the positions of the parties, the mediator will not only enable the parties to make a more objective risk analysis, but the mediator may also uncover a gap in understanding between the parties and their own counsel. By focusing on specific assessments, the mediator can move the parties toward a more realistic view of their cases and thereby greatly enhance the likelihood of settlement.

In caucus sessions, the mediator will ask parties to respond to an opponent's claim or defense or will demonstrate to the parties the weaknesses of their positions. In so doing, the mediator will explore weak points, consequences and areas of overconfidence with respect to both liability and damages. The mediator may ask questions which suggest that the facts or legal positions do not necessarily support the parties' conclusions. In addition, the mediator may remind the parties that the mediator is the only person in the room capable of making an objective assessment. Studies by leading programs on negotiation demonstrate that most parties and advocates tend to rely on the facts and law supporting their positions and give insufficient attention to the positions of the opposing party.

The mediator will ask the party to review the consequences of pursuing its position through litigation or arbitration. Any such discussion of the risks associated with litigation is likely to include costs, business disruption, loss of morale and productivity, burdens, discovery issues, timelines, possible appeals, jury uncertainties, judges' orientations, experts, witnesses' credibility and collectibility of any potential judgment.

### §4.6.10      Overcoming Irrational Assessments

When testing whether parties have made realistic evaluations of risk and exposure, a skilled mediator will determine whether the parties' evaluations have been affected by irrational biases or "cognitive illusions." The most common of these illusions are risk aversion, advocacy bias, certainty bias, hindsight bias and reactive devaluation. (*See* §6.8.11 Avoid Irrational Attachments to Positions for an explanation of these illusions). By sharing the conclusions reached by studies on cognitive illusions and biases (performed mostly in the past decade by graduate business schools and law schools), the mediator can help the parties overcome their irrational attachments to certain positions and make better settlement decisions. As discussed in the following section, a mediator can be particularly helpful working with the parties to overcome reactive devaluation.

### §4.6.11      Proposing Solutions to Overcome Reactive Devaluation

The theory of "reactive devaluation" suggests that a proposal may be considered acceptable, satisfactory, or attractive when proposed by one's own side but suspicious, unacceptable, or unattractive when proposed by an adverse party. A mediator can overcome reactive devaluation by offering one party's proposal to the other side as the mediator's own, so that the proposal may be received more openly. A mediator can also accomplish this result by suggesting a proposal in the form of a hypothetical.

## §4.6.12      Identifying and Overcoming Barriers to Resolution

Parties to disputes frequently run into obstacles when they try to resolve disputes in direct and unassisted negotiations. A skilled mediator, especially in separate caucus sessions, can work with the parties to identify these obstacles and develop strategies for resolution. The following chapter (Chapter 5 Negotiation and Mediation – Overcoming the Barriers to Resolution) discusses the common barriers to resolution and the techniques employed by the mediator to overcome them. These barriers are:

- selective perception in making evaluations

- wrong baselines

- reactive devaluation (*See* §4.6.11).

- failure to communicate

- gaps in information

- insufficient focus upon underlying interests

- inability to align client's interests

- disconnects between attorney and client

- anger and embarrassment

- behavior and tactics of parties and counsel

- poor negotiating skills

- inappropriate reliance on experts

- preoccupation with winning

- inability to break impasse (*See* §4.6.15)

- process barriers

### §4.6.13    Issuing an Evaluative Opinion

Because of the potential perception of bias, mediators rarely offer unsolicited opinions of value, litigation outcome or issue outcome without the agreement of the parties. Even solicited opinions are dangerous to the mediation process because of the potential for perceived bias. The mere appearance of bias can damage the integrity of the mediation process and impede or end progress. Such an opinion, however, may be appropriate if there is a deadlock in the negotiations.

### §4.6.14    "One Text" Approach to Reaching Agreement

In the "one text" approach, the mediator will draft a document of potential agreement. The mediator will then pass it back and forth or circulate it among the parties. As the text circulates and the concerns of the parties surface, the mediator will revise the text to reflect the parties' concerns. Where there is some common ground and, especially in an effort to restructure a relationship, this approach may be a good tool for reaching agreement. However, this technique does not work well where the only issue is the payment of a sum of money.

### §4.6.15    Impasse-Breaking Techniques

The skilled mediator will use a variety of techniques to break an initial impasse. Some methods include the basic tools of human psychology: the use of humor during a tense moment, the call for a recess, the creation of a new group dynamic by shifting the participants into different groups and the reconvening of all participants into a joint session. Other impasse-breaking techniques include refocusing on the importance of future relationships, reviewing the analysis of risk and cost, tracing the progress to date and acknowledging the possibility of an irreconcilable impasse so that the burden of breaking an impasse shifts to the parties themselves. Even when a real and ultimate impasse occurs, skilled mediators are well versed in a number of impasse breaking techniques, for example, adjournment, requesting a "last best" offer or using a double-blind proposal (*See* §5.2.14 Inability to Break Impasse).

## §4.7    MEDIATOR'S ROLE AT CONCLUSION

The mediator's role does not necessarily end at the conclusion of a mediation session. After the formal mediation sessions, there are certain understandings which should be reached among the parties, whether or not settlement has been reached at the conclusion of the process.

If agreement is reached, the mediator should insist that the parties execute a written settlement memorandum before the mediation session concludes. In some situations, the parties may also need a comprehensive written settlement agreement. In such an instance, the mediator will remain available to clarify misunderstandings and to help with unresolved issues and controversial provisions. The mediator also may offer to remain available to the parties to provide any other assistance which may be needed, including serving as a mediator or arbitrator of post-mediation disputes.

If agreement is not reached, the parties may want to address, either together or separately, the issue of the mediator's possible continuing efforts. Such involvement can often be a significant factor in producing a settlement.

## §4.8    ETHICAL STANDARDS FOR MEDIATORS

A number of professional organizations have enacted or are in the process of enacting codes of ethics for mediators. The American Arbitration Association, the ABA Section of Dispute Resolution, and SPIDR (now the Association for Conflict Resolution) have enacted Model Standards of Conduct for Mediators (*See* Appendix F). The CPR Georgetown Commission on Ethics and Standards in ADR (sponsored by Georgetown University and CPR Institute for Dispute Resolution) has drafted a Proposed Model Rule of Professional Conduct for the Lawyer as Third Party Neutral. The proposed Model Rule, which addresses the ethical responsibilities of lawyers serving as neutrals in mediations and other ADR proceedings, can be viewed on the website of the CPR Institute for Dispute Resolution at cpradr.org.

While ethical codes for mediators vary somewhat, they typically address the following issues confronting mediators:

- conflicts of interest

- competency

- impartiality

- legal advice

- informed consent

- advertising

- fees

Some mediators may be governed by the conduct of several codes; others may not be governed by any codes. In selecting a mediator, counsel should ask what code, if any, will govern the conduct of the mediator.

## §4.9    UNIFORM MEDIATION ACT

The American Bar Association House of Delegates, at its February 2002 meeting, voted to endorse the Uniform Mediation Act ("UMA"). The UMA is the result of a three-year collaborative effort by the ABA Section of Dispute Resolution, the National Conference of Commissioners on Uniform State Laws and academic scholars from numerous law schools. The UMA provides for the protection of confidentiality in mediation, requires disclosure by mediators of any potential conflicts of interest and provides for other standards to preserve the integrity of the mediation process. Although the UMA is now being introduced in state legislatures, and while it is of special interest for the numerous states that have no mediation statutes, the statute is not intended to replace existing state statutes providing even stronger protections than the minimum guarantees provided by the UMA.

# CHAPTER 5

## NEGOTIATION AND MEDIATION – OVERCOMING BARRIERS TO RESOLUTION

## §5.1    INTRODUCTION

Direct and unassisted negotiations can and should be considered as the initial path to resolving disputes. When successful, negotiation is the most flexible and cost-effective approach to resolving disputes whether or not litigation is pending. The negotiation process, however, depends upon the parties' ability to communicate, their willingness to make concessions and their ability to recognize possible solutions. Especially in substantial commercial disputes, the barriers to resolution often are so significant that parties will not even attempt a negotiated resolution or often will reach impasse if they do attempt to negotiate. A skilled mediator can often overcome the many obstacles that prevent negotiation from succeeding.

## §5.2 THE COMMON BARRIERS TO RESOLUTION

Below are the most common barriers to resolution in direct negotiations and an explanation of how a skilled and experienced mediator can overcome them.[1]

### §5.2.1 Selective Perception in Making Evaluations

Parties to a dispute and their counsel—both corporate counsel and outside counsel—invariably have difficulty making an objective evaluation of their own case. Recent studies by the Harvard Program on Negotiation and other institutions establish that self-interest and selective perception make it virtually impossible for any party or counsel to make a truly objective evaluation. Parties generally look for facts and law to support their own claims and overlook the evidence that might defeat their claims.

As Winston Churchill said, "Where you stand depends upon where you sit." A skilled mediator may be the only person in the room who can make a truly objective evaluation and act as an agent of reality. While mediation is a facilitative process, especially in its beginning stages, mediators can appropriately challenge parties to consider whether their assessments are realistic without offering their own opinions on the merits.

---

[1]     This Chapter is adapted from an article by the author entitled "Breaking Down Barriers In Negotiation Through Mediation," December 2001 edition of *Alternatives*, published by the CPR Institute for Dispute Resolution.

## §5.2.2      Wrong Baselines

Parties in a negotiation commonly compare what is on the table with what they want or need or with what they consider to be fair. A skilled mediator can work with the parties to have them make a real world comparison–one that compares what is on the table to the consequences that will occur in the absence of a negotiated resolution. A skilled mediator can challenge the parties to compare any offer with their BATNA, or *best alternative to a negotiated agreement*, and WATNA, or *worst alternative to a negotiated agreement*. These become the baselines for what parties should accept or reject. Moreover, within these baselines, a skilled mediator will continually challenge parties to make realistic assessments.

## §5.2.3      Reactive Devaluation

It is common for a party to reject a proposal made by an adversary if for no reason other than the fact that it was proposed by the adversary. Parties often are unable to assess the accuracy of information or accept a settlement proposal as made in good faith because they distrust the source. This phenomenon is known as "reactive devaluation." A skilled mediator can overcome this phenomenon by presenting proposals as his or her own or by simply floating hypothetical proposals. After learning the disputants' general settlement parameters, a mediator often can float proposals likely to work for all parties.

## §5.2.4      Failure to Communicate

In some cases, parties litigate for years without any communications about settlement. Notwithstanding communications about pleadings, motions, discovery and hearings, many litigators focus on trial preparation and strategy to the exclusion of settlement. Many lawyers avoid settlement initiatives to dispel any suggestion of weakness. Settlement can occur–sometimes rather easily—if the parties communicate earlier and more openly. I have acted as a mediator in a few cases where there were not only the usual "gaps" between the parties, but there were unrecognized "overlaps."

In one case, a plaintiff stated that while it would accept $800,000 to settle its claim, the defendant would, in the plaintiff's view, pay only $500,000. The defendant confided that it would pay $900,000 to resolve the dispute, but it was certain the plaintiff would not settle for less than $1 million. Thus, there was an unrecognized $100,000 overlap. In this instance, both parties had made realistic assessments about value, but inaccurate assessments about the other side's settlement position. A skilled mediator can facilitate good communication about settlement in cases where the parties are reluctant to do so on their own.

### §5.2.5    Gaps in Information

Information gaps often present barriers to resolution. In preparing for mediation sessions, a skilled mediator will recognize the existence of such gaps and encourage the other side to provide information, such as an accounting, that supports a claim for damages, or case law that supports an important legal position. Information exchanges can help parties resolve disputes on their own. In one case involving a professional partnership dispute, the voluntary submission of an accounting resulted in the withdrawal of all claims and the termination of the dispute. Similarly, mediators are in a good position to clarify misunderstandings concerning the information provided or positions taken by either side.

### §5.2.6    Insufficient Focus Upon Underlying Interests

Many parties engage in "distributive bargaining" in which they exchange offers and demands in an effort to "divide the pie." As a consequence, these parties fail to capture an opportunity to create value. In contrast, a skilled mediator will encourage the parties to engage in "integrative bargaining" and take a more collaborative approach to negotiations. Parties are encouraged to focus upon their interests as well as their rights and look for business-driven solutions. For example, distribution agreements can be restructured to provide for new provisions on territoriality or exclusivity. Supply agreements can be restructured to provide for future price discounts. If there is a continuing relationship, the parties will be asked to compare and contrast the issues in dispute with the importance of the relationship itself. Even in pure monetary disputes, parties can provide for creative means of monetary exchange. While much has been written about the potential for "win-win" in mediation, the possibility of such a result is not purely theoretical. I have participated in numerous mediations where all parties have viewed a settlement to be *better* than their probable best result in litigation (taking into account the risks, costs and distractions of litigation).

### §5.2.7      Inability to Align Client's Interests

Many parties and their inside and outside counsel perceive a dispute as having only one dimension. In a typical dispute between two parties, the focus of negotiations will be primarily upon differing views between the parties as to facts, claims, defenses, rights, obligations, experts, damages, issues of credibility and outcomes. A more sophisticated analysis also will include the objectives, interests and needs of the parties. This one-dimensional approach ignores the possibility that the problem may have more to do with differences among and between the various constituent representatives of the client than differences between the parties. In one mediation, for example, the principal settlement obstacle was a disagreement about which division's profit-and-loss statement would be "hit" by a substantial payment to the plaintiff. In another, the principal obstacle was a disagreement about when to settle, given the fact that a settlement would require the company to restate its earnings. A skilled mediator will recognize such problems and be in a position to conduct an intramural mediation between the client's representatives so that they can be aligned on settlement goals and positions.

### §5.2.8      Disconnects Between Attorney and Client

A one-dimensional approach to a dispute (focusing solely upon differences between the parties) also ignores the fact that differences between an attorney and the client can create barriers to resolution. In many mediations, parties are unprepared to make realistic assessments because counsel has overstated the likelihood of success at the outset of a dispute or failed to communicate with the client on an adequate basis. Conversely, counsel may make a fairly reasonable litigation-risk assessment—only to have the client refuse to accept bad news. In a recent dispute, upon hearing the opinion of counsel, the president of a fairly large company stated to his own attorney, "I thought you were *my* lawyer."

In another dispute, at the conclusion of a successful mediation, an attorney privately said to me, "Thank you for telling my client what I could not say to him." Contingent fees also may present barriers to resolution. In one such dispute, counsel for the plaintiffs argued against a settlement the client was otherwise prepared to accept because the settlement would not produce a sufficient return on counsel's investment of time. Mediators are in a good position to discern and deal with any disconnect between attorney and client.

### §5.2.9    Anger and Embarrassment

It is not uncommon for business representatives to become angry or hostile to their counterparts in a failed business transaction or venture. Similarly, long-term partners and family members often stop speaking to one another as the result of differences of opinion in running the business. This hostility often prevents the parties from being able to jointly negotiate a resolution. A skilled mediator can provide a forum in which to facilitate communication and permit the parties to vent, overcome anger and recognize the need for closure. In "angry" disputes, an apology can serve as a linchpin for resolution and, in some cases, a predicate for a rehabilitated relationship. Parties also can become entrenched in their settlement positions, especially where they draw a "line in the sand" in negotiations at an early stage of a dispute. Many parties, even in the face of new information, become too embarrassed to change their positions. A skilled mediator can present new information and facilitate negotiations in ways that enable parties to change their positions and save face.

### §5.2.10    Behavior and Tactics of Parties and Counsel

In direct negotiations, parties and counsel often will behave poorly and engage in conduct destructive to the negotiation process. Threats to walk away, assertions of lack of authority, nonnegotiable demands and intimidation are just a few examples of the tactics or tricks that can derail direct negotiations between parties. The mere presence of a mediator usually alters such behavior. In a mediation, parties and counsel are usually on good behavior as they want to convince the mediator that their conduct giving rise to the dispute was responsible. They also want to convince the mediator that their approaches to the negotiations are both fair and reasonable. In any event, the mediator is in a far better position than the parties to develop approaches and strategies that minimize the significance of such tactics.

### §5.2.11      Poor Negotiating Skills

Well over 90% of all cases in litigation are resolved prior to trial. While most litigators are well trained in advocacy and trial skills, they approach negotiations on a somewhat intuitive basis. It is not at all surprising, therefore, that many lawyers find it difficult to resolve a case until the ultimate imperative arrives–the looming trial date. Parties and counsel often approach settlement negotiations with a firm view of what they want or need, but without any consideration of what they might have to accept – their bottom line. Parties and counsel commonly make a thorough analysis of their own rights and interests, but often fail to make a significant analysis of the other side's perspectives and interests. In most negotiations, advocates are far too focused on trying to convince the other side of the strength of their positions and insufficiently attentive to what the other side is saying. Many parties are unwilling to make a significant move in a negotiation because they subscribe to the conventional wisdom that "a party should not bid against itself."

Most highly skilled mediators are well versed in the art and science of negotiations. Training and experience permits a skilled mediator to assist parties with their negotiating strategies and decisions. For example, notwithstanding the conventional wisdom that parties should not bid against themselves, a skilled mediator can show parties how they can anchor a negotiation in *their* zone by making the "first credible offer." Mediators can also set a stage for parties to listen to each other carefully and respectfully. As suggested earlier, mediators can urge parties to make more objective evaluations and to compare proposals not to abstract wish lists, but to the consequences should settlement negotiations fail.

### §5.2.12      Inappropriate Reliance on Experts

In many disputes, parties develop hardline positions in negotiations due to a heavy reliance on their own experts. Given the late stage in the litigation process at which expert reports are exchanged, parties can be unaware for years of the positions of their adversary's experts. A skilled mediator can provide for an early, informal exchange of opinions by experts. These exchanges can occur even before experts have formed their final opinions or offered their written reports. In several cases, I have conducted what can be characterized as a "minitrial within a mediation." These mediations featured an informal, mediator-moderated exchange of experts' opinions, where the experts have had a limited opportunity to state their conclusions and to pose questions to each other. In these "minitrials," attorneys and clients attending the mediation have merely observed this controlled exchange. In each case, the opportunity to observe an exchange of the views of experts has resulted in a softening of hardline settlement positions and served as a predicate to resolution.

### §5.2.13    Preoccupation With Winning

Many companies commence litigation upon a belief that they have been wronged in a commercial transaction. Upon being served with a complaint, many companies perceive that they have been wrongfully attacked and, at least initially, adopt a win-at-any-cost approach. Business persons directly involved in the transaction at the core of the litigation often urge their key executives to seek a declaration of rights in order to be vindicated. While many larger companies have institutionalized ADR, the support from within is often neither very broad nor very deep. Moreover, smaller and more entrepreneurial companies rarely involved in litigation are even less inclined to compromise (at least initially) and often view the need to prosecute or defend a suit to be a matter of principle. In mediation, a skilled mediator can get the parties to recognize that not every case should be interpreted as a matter of principle. As one legal analyst stated: "Every case is a matter of 'principle' until the client receives the third and fourth bill from outside counsel at which time they will begin to spell the word differently ('principal')."

In addition, a skilled mediator often will be successful in convincing parties that they need to focus not upon what happened, but upon the evidence a court will hear. While parties often want to litigate to establish the truth, a skilled mediator can suggest why they can only hope for "court truth" as distinct from "absolute truth." Ultimately, the mediator's challenge is to urge the parties to take a more bottom-line approach in pursuit of their claims and defenses. By examining all of the relevant considerations and viewing the dispute as a problem to be solved, most parties will realize that their most responsible decision will be one that involves some compromise.

### §5.2.14        Inability to Break Impasse

Parties who elect to engage in the process of direct and unassisted negotiations often find it difficult to overcome an impasse on their own. Skilled mediators recognize the first signals of approaching impasse when they hear statements such as "This is my bottom line," or "I knew this would be a waste of time," or "We are leaving." A skilled mediator can also detect early signs of possible impasse from the nonverbal conduct of the parties. Skilled mediators are particularly adept at determining whether the "impasse" is a matter of posturing or whether it is real. If the perceived impasse occurs as a consequence of posturing between the parties or by a party with the mediator, mediators use a number of techniques to generate movement and overcome the problem. Even when a real and ultimate impasse occurs, skilled mediators are well versed in a number of impasse breaking techniques, for example, adjournment, requesting a "last-best" offer proposal, or using a double-blind proposal. In such an instance, the proposal is made to each side confidentially for their acceptance or rejection. Unless both accept, a party will not know whether the other side has accepted the proposal.

### §5.2.15        Process Barriers

Each of the above paragraphs illuminates the barriers to resolution in party-to-party negotiations and the ways in which a mediator can overcome them. In addition to the techniques, skills, and strategies that a mediator brings to the process, the simple fact that there is an event — the mediation itself — enhances the potential for resolution. In many cases, parties are simply not ready to resolve a dispute in direct negotiations because of their need for a day in court. Mediation can provide the needed "day in court" by giving the parties an opportunity to tell their story and get feedback from a neutral. Moreover, in mediation, parties are better prepared for negotiations and are required to make decisions within a defined time frame. Further, in direct negotiations parties often need approval to settle at levels beyond their authorization or are concerned about the need for cover in order that their settlement decisions not be criticized at higher levels within the organization. Recommendations or feedback from a mediator often can satisfy these needs and concerns. Finally, in direct negotiations it is easy to blame the other side for any failure to achieve resolution. In contrast, parties in mediation are likely to become invested in the process and work harder to achieve a resolution; achieving resolution becomes a part of the definition of "success."

## §5.3    FURTHER READING ON BARRIERS IN NEGOTIATIONS

Chapter 5's discussion of the barriers in negotiations is based upon the author's personal experiences in mediation. There are a number of important works that examine similar barriers in negotiations from a more theoretical perspective. Among these are Robert Mnookin's diagnostic approach, which identifies four classic barriers to agreement: cognitive, strategic, principal-agent and reactive devaluation. *See* Robert H. Mnookin, *Why Negotiations Fail: An Exploration of Barriers to the Resolution of Conflict*, 8 Ohio State Journal on Dispute Resolution 235 (1993). Christopher Moore, in his "Circle of Conflict," identifies conflicts as emanating from data, interests, structure, values or relationships. *See* Christopher W. Moore, *The Mediation Process* 27, Jossey-Bass Publishers (1986).

Any critical analysis of the negotiation process also must recognize the effectiveness of a problem-solving approach, in contrast to a more competitive approach focused upon winning. Carrie Menkel-Meadow addresses the benefits to be achieved by parties crafting solutions to expand the available resources and meet the needs of the parties. *See* Carrie Menkel-Meadow, *Toward Another View of Legal Negotiation: The Structure of Problem Solving*, 31 UCLA L. Rev. 754 (1984).

Gerry Williams' analytical approach identifies the five steps for recovering from conflict (denial, acceptance, sacrifice, leap of faith and renewal). Drawing upon the literature in law, psychology, anthropology and related disciplines, he discusses the potential for the disputants to be transformed by the process. *See* Gerald R. Williams, *Negotiation as a Healing Process*, 1996 J. Disp. Resol. 1.

## §5.4    CONCLUSION

Whatever the barriers to resolution, good mediators bring to the table an understanding of the social psychology of negotiations and an appreciation for how parties perceive and deal with the issue of risk. Highly skilled mediators are well versed in mediation techniques like paraphrasing, framing and the use of mediator transparency. They also know how to manage the process when a party is not acting in good faith or where there is an imbalance of power. The best mediators apply leadership and problem-solving skills and earn the trust of the parties. Ultimately, they will involve the parties directly in the search for solutions. While direct and unassisted negotiation should remain the initial path to dispute resolution, where some of the above barriers appear to be an impediment, parties should recognize the benefits of a facilitated negotiation with the help of a skilled and experienced mediator.

# CHAPTER 6

## PREPARING FOR MEDIATION

## 6.1    INTRODUCTION

In order to take full advantage of the opportunities presented by mediation, the mediation advocate needs to understand the mediation process and be completely prepared. Since mediation is non-binding, some attorneys erroneously assume that there is no downside and that the preparation needed for a mediation is minimal. In fact, the lawyer who understands how to advance a client's interest by influencing the design of the process and by properly preparing the representative of the client will gain significant advantages in mediation. Good preparation is as much a key to success in mediation as it is in litigation.

This chapter suggests strategies that will enable mediation counsel to maximize the opportunities offered to a client in a mediation.

## §6.2    STEP-BY-STEP MEDIATION ANALYSIS

The following chart provides an overview of the mediation process. From the outset of a dispute, counsel should take a view of the big picture—the entire mediation process—in order to take full advantage of the process.

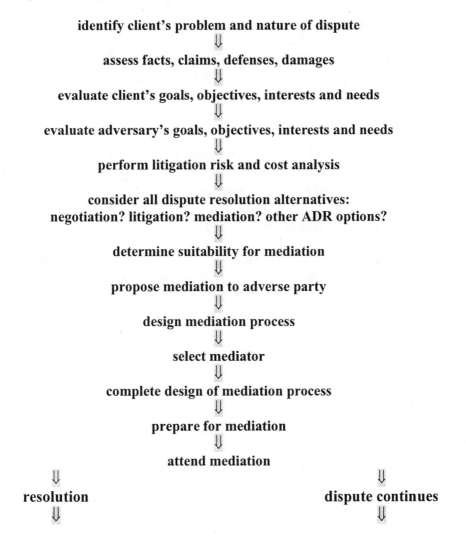

**identify client's problem and nature of dispute**
⇓
**assess facts, claims, defenses, damages**
⇓
**evaluate client's goals, objectives, interests and needs**
⇓
**evaluate adversary's goals, objectives, interests and needs**
⇓
**perform litigation risk and cost analysis**
⇓
**consider all dispute resolution alternatives:**
**negotiation? litigation? mediation? other ADR options?**
⇓
**determine suitability for mediation**
⇓
**propose mediation to adverse party**
⇓
**design mediation process**
⇓
**select mediator**
⇓
**complete design of mediation process**
⇓
**prepare for mediation**
⇓
**attend mediation**

⇓                                     ⇓
**resolution**                              **dispute continues**
⇓                                     ⇓

⇓

**prepare written settlement
agreement if parties
resolve dispute**

⇓

**consider alternatives
if mediation does not
resolve dispute**

## §6.3 MAKE AN OBJECTIVE LITIGATION-RISK ANALYSIS

To determine the client's negotiating strategy in mediation and establish benchmarks for settlement, counsel should assess the likely outcomes and probable costs of a dispute in litigation (or arbitration). Any litigation-risk analysis should include the following assessments:

- evaluate the strengths and weaknesses of client's case including assessment of legal arguments and credibility of witnesses and evidence

- evaluate the strengths and weaknesses of opponent's case

- determine the best and worst possible outcomes of a litigated resolution (consider a "decision-tree" approach to this analysis)

- estimate client costs of litigation, including discovery, motions, witness preparation, expert fees and trial costs

- consider the transactional costs to client, including time away from the conduct of normal business, impact on morale and loss of productivity

- assess the probable timelines in litigation, including any appeals

- assess the financial condition of the adverse party and determine whether there are any collectability problems

## §6.4    ANALYZE THE INTERESTS OF ALL PARTIES

The underlying interests are often as compelling (sometimes more compelling) as the rights and obligations of the parties when making a settlement analysis and developing a negotiating strategy for mediation. Any analysis of the underlying interests should include the following assessments:

- What are the goals and objectives of the client? What does the client really need?

- What are the goals and objectives of all other parties? What do they really need?

- Do the underlying interests present any specific reason why mediation (or early resolution) may be particularly attractive?

- Is there any need or potential to preserve a relationship?

- Does any party have a particular need for confidentiality?

- Does the existence of the dispute create a morale problem for any party?

- Does the pending dispute create an impediment to a party's strategic plans?

- What impact will a settlement have on a company's bottom line? On its reported earnings? On a division's budget?

- What issues are most important to each party? Least important?

Appendix K (Negotiation Plan for Dispute Resolution in Litigation) offers a template for making the litigation-risk and interests analysis as discussed in this and preceding section.

## §6.5 COUNSEL THE CLIENT ON THE DECISION TO MEDIATE

In evaluating whether a dispute should be mediated, (*See* §2.2 Suitability of Dispute for Mediation), counsel should explore the following questions with the client:

- Is a settlement possible?

- What are the likely barriers to a settlement?

- Is it too soon for settlement to occur?

- Is more information required before a settlement decision can be made and, if so, can the parties agree to exchange this information as part of a mediation agreement?

- Are there other claims or potential disputes not yet involved in the case or controversy that can also be resolved in a mediation?

- Are emotions or hostilities likely to bar the kind of communication necessary to settle a dispute? If so, is it possible that the mediation will provide an appropriate forum for better communication?

- Are there additional stakeholders in the dispute that may be willing to participate in settlement discussions?

- Are all parties to the dispute willing to engage in a good faith effort to resolve the dispute?

Once the answers to these questions have been reviewed, the client can review the factors outlined in §2.2 (Suitability of Dispute for Mediation) and make an informed decision about whether mediation will best serve its interests.

## §6.6    SELECT THE MEDIATOR

After making the decision to mediate, counsel should determine what type of mediator is best suited for the client and the particular dispute. Counsel should then find the candidate with the appropriate expertise, style and other desired qualities. Each party may submit a list of candidates for the opponent's review or the parties may retain a neutral ADR service to recommend a mediator for their consideration. Among the organizations prepared to recommend mediator candidates in business disputes are the CPR Institute for Dispute Resolution, the American Arbitration Association and JAMS. Organizations such as the American College of Civil Trial Mediators and the International Academy of Mediators also offer, on their websites, the credentials of mediators highly skilled and experienced in mediating commercial disputes. When turning to an ADR organization to administer the selection process, parties should inform the organization of any preferences in mediation style, experience, expertise, or location of candidates.

Counsel should take the selection process seriously and take the time to engage in due diligence. A competent advocate should learn as much as possible about mediator candidates by obtaining their credentials and references, researching community reputation and speaking to the candidates directly. It is entirely appropriate to ask candidates specific questions about their experience, style and expertise (*See* §4.2 Qualities of an Effective Mediator).

Since initial private conversations with a mediator candidate may create the appearance of bias, especially if there are lengthy conversations of substance, it may be advisable to schedule an initial joint conference with a mediator candidate and opposing counsel for the purpose of interviewing a particular candidate.

The following factors should be considered in the selection process:

- personal qualities of an effective mediator (*See* §4.2)

- mediation style and approach

  - facilitative or evaluative
  - broad or narrow
  - passive or active
  - combined

- expertise

  - subject matter
  - technical
  - legal

- mediation experience

- availability of mediator

- the mediator's professional fees and administrative charges

- how and when the mediator uses caucus sessions

- whether the mediator encourages lawyer participation

- whether the mediator will involve the parties directly

- how the mediator uses reality testing techniques

- the circumstances in which the mediator will offer an evaluative opinion

- whether the mediator requires pre-mediation documentation and submissions

- any conflict of interest or reason the mediator may not be absolutely impartial

- restrictions on future representations, if mediator is a practicing lawyer

- references from lawyers and parties in similar disputes

- the code of ethics that will govern the mediator's conduct

Once the mediator is selected, the parties should enter into a written agreement with the mediator covering issues such as the mediation process, confidentiality, conflicts of interest and pricing (*See* Appendices G and H).

## §6.7    PARTICIPATE WITH MEDIATOR IN DESIGNING THE PROCESS

The mediator, especially in more substantial or complex disputes, can assist counsel in preparing for the mediation. For example, the mediator can help determine what type of negotiating approach will be most effective, whether to have experts attend the mediation sessions or whether visual aids might be helpful. While *ex parte* contacts are entirely appropriate, it is important that they be disclosed in a general way and balanced overall in order that the mediator be perceived by the parties as absolutely impartial.

The following is a list of the important procedural issues to discuss with the mediator:

- dates and times

- location

- available facilities

- anticipated length of process

- exchange of information

- participants

- written submissions

- oral presentations

- administrative and professional fees

- confidentiality

In planning for the mediation sessions, the participants should set aside sufficient time. It is not uncommon in the mediation of a dispute involving substantial dollars or interests for the process to take two days or longer. In substantial commercial cases, mediators commonly will ask the participants to set aside two or more consecutive days and to be prepared to stay into the evenings, if necessary.

## §6.8   PREPARE FOR THE MEDIATION SESSION

### §6.8.1   Importance of Preparation

Preparation is essential for an effective mediation. Lawyers often participate in a mediation without a full understanding of the dispute or the process. With good preparation, a lawyer can significantly enhance the likelihood of a positive outcome for the client.

### §6.8.2   Comparison of Preparation for Mediation with Preparation for Litigation

Preparation for a mediation is different from preparing for a deposition or a trial. The following important differences should be considered when preparing for a mediation:

- *Role of the client*—Unlike litigation, in mediation the client is directly involved and plays a pivotal role. The client, therefore, should also be central in the preparation stage. The client needs to be prepared for its roles as a presenter of information, a negotiator and a decision maker.

- *Discovery*—If information is necessary to evaluate the merits of the case or reasonable settlement options, counsel should determine how such information should be obtained and whether formal discovery is necessary. The parties may agree to bypass formal discovery and voluntarily exchange information either before or during the mediation process. For example, defendants are often unprepared to resolve claims in mediation without having received damage information in advance of the mediation session. The mediator's assistance should be enlisted in the event an agreement on voluntary exchange cannot be obtained.

- *Mediation submissions*—Written submissions afford an opportunity to convince the mediator of the correctness of a client's position or the reasonableness of a particular settlement option. These submissions also afford an opportunity to address the client's underlying interests and objectives. They should be drafted with care and professionalism.

- *Rules of evidence*—Rules of evidence do not apply in mediation. Counsel should be aware that although witnesses and demonstrative aids may be useful, there is no formal direct or cross-examination. A mediator may, however, request that a party explain his or her statements and perspectives or react to what an opponent has asserted. Witness preparation, therefore, is as important in mediation as it is in litigation.

- *Mediation session*—In preparing legal arguments or settlement proposals to be presented at the mediation session, counsel should recognize that the process affords an opportunity to make presentations to representatives of the parties as well as to the mediator. This approach is different from litigation, where statements are addressed to a judge or jury.

- *Negotiations*—Mediation, as a negotiating process, is a less adversarial and more cooperative process than litigation. While arguments should be presented persuasively, counsel should avoid the use of emotionally charged language and should acknowledge the other parties' concerns, where appropriate. At times, the atmosphere of a mediation is not unlike an oral argument in court and, at times, not unlike the negotiation of a business deal.

### §6.8.3   Identify the Client Representatives Who Should Participate

To maximize the opportunities presented by mediation, it is important to identify the client representatives who will take ownership of the dispute. While the participation of individuals with knowledge of facts giving rise to a controversy may or may not advance the client's interests, it is more important to encourage the participation of a decision maker with full authority to make resolution decisions, including the impact any such decision may have on a division's budget or the company's reported earnings. Counsel should make every effort to identify and encourage the appropriate client representatives to participate in mediation in order to have the best opportunity to recognize potential solutions and to assure that any settlement decision is made with full appreciation of the risks and likely outcomes in litigation.

### §6.8.4   Consider Alternatives to Negotiated Agreement (BATNA and WATNA)

Before beginning formal negotiations, counsel should help the client explore alternatives should negotiations fail – the *best and worst alternatives to a negotiated agreement* (BATNA and WATNA). *See* Fisher, Roger and William Ury, *Getting To Yes: Negotiating Agreement Without Giving In* (Houghton Mifflin Co. 1981). By examining various alternatives, the client and counsel can jointly determine whether or not any settlement being offered in mediation is in the client's best interests. A viable, well-developed alternative to a negotiated settlement gives the client the power to negotiate from a position of strength. Counsel should specifically assist the client in determining its *best alternative to a negotiated agreement*—BATNA. Any offer that is better than a party's BATNA should be accepted.

Assessing whether the opposing party has a strong or weak BATNA also helps in understanding its position and negotiating strengths. The more the advocate knows about his or her opponent's alternatives, the better prepared he or she is to negotiate a successful resolution.

Counsel should also assist the client in developing its *worst alternative to a negotiated agreement*—WATNA. Defining the WATNA protects the client from accepting an inadequate settlement offer. Used in conjunction with the BATNA, it is another tool for recognizing when to accept or reject a settlement offer. Having worked out the BATNA and WATNA prior to negotiations, the advocate will have more control throughout the mediation process. At the same time, however, parties should be open to the possibility that their BATNA and WATNA can change as a result of what they learn in the mediation process.

### §6.8.5    Prepare Arguments Supporting Legal Positions and Settlement Proposals

Counsel should prepare arguments supporting the merits of claims and defenses in the same manner as when preparing for trial. Counsel should be able to demonstrate to the mediator and opposing parties the strengths of the client's case and weaknesses of the opponent's case. Counsel should also prepare in advance any reason why the other side should be willing to move to a "reasonable" settlement proposal. Here, the advocate's goal is to persuade the other side to consider his or her client's proposal. Accordingly, counsel should recognize and be prepared to advance reasons why the other side's interests are being served by a specific settlement proposal.

### §6.8.6    Explore Creative Solutions

To remain open to creative solutions, the mediation advocate should look at the case from the perspective of all parties. Together with the client, counsel should determine the interests, objectives, concerns and needs of each party. Brainstorming with the client will enhance the possibility of recognizing possible creative solutions that work for all parties to the dispute.

### §6.8.7 Prepare for Client's Direct Involvement

Since clients often become directly involved in the mediation process, they must be fully prepared for this role. Counsel should meet with the representatives of the client before the mediation to discuss the mediation process, the client's involvement and issues such as format, procedure, demeanor and dress. In short, the representative of the client should know what to expect so that the client is comfortable and well prepared for his or her role as a presenter of information and a negotiator.

### §6.8.8 Decide Who Should Take Lead in Sessions

Counsel and the client representative should determine together who should take the lead role during the mediation sessions—the advocate or the client representative. To make this determination, counsel should consider the client representative's sophistication, ability to articulate goals, knowledge of the subject matter, ability for constructive expression and the advisability of the client's active participation. If the client representative is a persuasive and effective communicator, the client has an advantage that should be used in the mediation. It is also important to recognize that the client's participation gives the adverse party a preview of how well the client representative will perform as a witness in court. In general, the more a client participates, the more satisfied the client is with the process and the outcome.

### §6.8.9 Explore Potential for Collaborative Negotiations

Whether negotiating directly with an adversary or in a mediation setting, movement often depends upon the willingness of the parties to cooperate. For example, counsel should consider what information needs to be exchanged to evaluate reasonable settlement options. Counsel may then agree voluntarily to exchange such information. Working with the opposing party in a cooperative manner demonstrates the advocate's good faith commitment to the process of a negotiated resolution.

Though the mediation advocate should be committed to a good faith effort to resolve the dispute, he or she nevertheless must represent the client energetically and persuasively. The advocate should argue convincingly on behalf of the client and be cautious of compromising too much too soon. However, in mediation, the lawyer must balance zealous advocacy with good negotiating techniques. Counsel should understand the interests and goals of his or her client and the opposing party. Counsel also should avoid emotional language in an effort to minimize antagonism and create a path for settlement.

### §6.8.10    Develop a Negotiating Plan

Whether the parties are engaged in a "pure dollars" dispute or one that involves the potential for a business solution, counsel and the client should prepare a negotiating plan in advance of the mediation. All too often, parties lose significant advantages in mediation as the result of having planned only initial offers and demands and tentative final positions.

Many mediations begin with the parties taking extreme positions, often representing the last offers and demands in settlement negotiations proceeding the mediation. Initially, parties often find themselves at an impasse as the result of their unwillingness to bid against themselves. In these circumstances, counsel should consider the advantages of making the first credible move. Even a small move, if credible, may enable the mediator to meet with the other side and gain significant concessions. (*See* §7.4.5 Demands and Offers).

In recognition of the fact that counsel and the client will be engaged in a "negotiation" with the mediator as well as adverse parties, counsel should plan the extent of voluntary candor with the mediator. The degree of voluntary candor may depend on a number of factors, including whether the mediator is more facilitative or evaluative; whether the communication involves legal arguments, underlying interests or settlement positions; and whether the mediation is in its early or late stages (*See* §4.5 The Mediator As Negotiator). In the final analysis, this judgment call is likely to depend on the level of comfort with the mediator and be made in the fluid environment of the mediation sessions.

In developing a negotiating plan, counsel should consider the following:

- litigation risk and cost benefit analysis

- client's interests, goals and objectives

- both sides' BATNA and WATNA

- the other side's business operations and corporate culture

- possible creative paths toward settlement

- possible collaborative negotiating strategies

- client's opening position

- advantage of first credible move

- offers contingent upon movement by other side

- possible counter-offers and responses

- rationale to support negotiating positions

- preparation of chart for tracking offers and counter-offers during negotiations

- suggestions for mediator in event of impasse

- plan for "negotiating" with mediator

While a specific negotiating plan is essential, counsel should recognize the need for flexibility in the mediation sessions and should be prepared to reevaluate the plan in light of new information received and the mediator's suggestions.

### § 6.8.11   Avoid Irrational Attachment to Positions

When preparing for mediation, most parties establish benchmarks for settlement in advance of the process. In disputes primarily about money, after assessing the likely risks and costs of litigation, most parties identify settlement ranges and many establish "bottom lines." Invariably, these assessments are influenced by irrational attachments to positions, sometimes referred to as "cognitive illusions," which produce errors in judgment that impact settlement decisions. Parties and counsel, therefore, when establishing benchmarks for settlement, should make every effort to determine whether any of the following cognitive illusions (or biases) have affected their evaluations or decisions about settlement.

• *Risk aversion.* Studies on negotiation have established that parties make different decisions about risk depending upon whether they categorize (or "frame") the risk as a gain or a loss. Usually from the reference point of the status quo, most parties are risk-averse when protecting settlements regarded as "gains" and are risk-seeking when making decisions involving results regarded as "losses." For example, most "plaintiffs" would prefer receiving $100,000 (a "gain") to a 50% chance of a verdict of $200,000. On the other hand, most "defendants" would prefer a 50% chance of a verdict of $200,000 to a payment (or "loss") of $100,000.

• *Advocacy bias.* Most parties and counsel have difficulty overcoming self-serving judgments about the likelihood of success on the merits in litigation (or arbitration). The bias results from selective perception and the fact that most parties identify the strengths of their case, but pay insufficient attention to or discredit possible weaknesses. In one study on advocacy bias, given the same set of facts and an instruction to make an objective evaluation of a case in order to provide the client with a benchmark to assist in making settlement decisions, participating "plaintiffs" found in favor of plaintiffs and for substantially higher amounts than did participating "defendants."

• *Certainty bias.* Studies on negotiations have established that most people overestimate their degree of certainty when answering questions or making assessments about probable outcomes in litigation. As a group, lawyers are particularly likely to overestimate their degree of certainty. This bias should be examined when making settlement recommendations and decisions, particularly when predicting the likely result at trial on a percentage basis. Given the uncertainty in litigation, it is difficult to predict outcomes in litigation in exact percentages in contrast to a range of percentages.

• *Hindsight bias.* Parties and counsel invariably overestimate the predictability of past events and fail to recognize, when making predictions, that hindsight is twenty-twenty. As a consequence, the assessment of whether or not conduct is wrongful is likely to be determined differently by one person making an objective decision before the fact and another person (or jury) assessing, after the fact, whether conduct was wrongful and, if so, whether actual damage resulted from alleged wrongful conduct. For example, a decision that it is not necessary to adopt a safety measure will be viewed more critically after the fact, in the context of a trial to determine whether the failure to take the precaution caused actual harm.

• *Reactive devaluation.* Parties and counsel often will discredit information or reject a proposal from an adversary solely because of the fact that it was proposed by the adversary – a phenomenon known as "reactive devaluation." (*See* §5.2.3 Reactive Devaluation).

Because of the above irrational attachments to positions (or cognitive illusions), it is difficult for parties and counsel to make completely objective assessments about either outcomes in litigation or settlement. Settlements are far more rational when parties make an effort to recognize whether any of the above cognitive illusions or biases have influenced their assessments.

A more thorough analysis of the above issues, including studies on principles of cognitive illusions, can be found in Chris Guthrie, Jeffrey J. Rachlinski & Andrew J. Winstrich, *Inside the Judicial Mind*, 86 Cornell Law Review 4 (May 2001).

### §6.8.12    Checklist of Questions for Client

The following is a checklist of questions to review with the client in preparing for a mediation:

• What was the sequence of events—facts?

• What business interests are involved in this dispute?

- How do you feel about this dispute? How does the other side feel about the dispute?

- What do you want/need?

- What is most important?

- What is least important?

- What do you believe are the strengths and weaknesses of your case?

- What do you believe are the strengths and weaknesses of your opponent's case?

- What alternatives would you consider if agreement cannot be reached?

- What is the most attractive alternative?

- What is the least attractive alternative?

- How would you prioritize the alternatives?

- What are your bottom-line monetary recovery needs?

- What are your non-monetary needs?

- What are your settlement expectations?

- What compromises will you consider to reach a negotiated settlement?

- What are you unwilling to compromise under any circumstances?

- What do you believe are the opposing party's interests, goals and objectives in the dispute?

- Can you prioritize the opposing party's interests?

- What is the opposing party's interest in a negotiated settlement?

- Are you interested in privacy or do you prefer a public forum?

- Are you interested in a speedy resolution?

- Do you have an interest in preserving a continuing relationship with the opposing party?

- Do you have any contracts or relationships with the opposing party which are not the subject of this dispute?

- What are the barriers to a settlement?

- Do you believe that emotions or hostilities will be a barrier to settlement?

- Who are the decision makers for the other side?

- How would you describe the personalities of the other side's decision makers?

- Are there any other potential parties with an interest, who, if notified, would increase the likelihood of serious negotiations taking place?

- Who should be participating directly in the presentation of the case? The negotiations?

- What particular concerns do you have about mediating this dispute?

## §6.9    PROTECT CONFIDENTIALITY

Confidentiality is a cornerstone of the mediation process. Generally, confidentiality is protected and defined by several sources—evidence codes, statutes, contract, the mediator and third-party provider rules and procedures. However, since the protections of confidentiality are far from absolute, counsel should understand the sometimes confusing distinction between "confidentiality" and "privilege" and take affirmative measures to secure the maximum level of protection for the client.

While Federal Rule of Evidence 408 and many state counterparts may give significant protection for statements made in compromise negotiations, the rules of evidence cover only what is admitted and excluded at trial and are not guarantees of confidentiality. For example, the rule does not bar an adverse party from using a mediation statement in a subsequent deposition. Nor does the rule limit the use of a statement in an arbitration, in the press or in public.

The "privilege" created by state statutes typically provides a much broader scope of protection for statements made during the course of a mediation. State statutes also protect the mediator from being called as a witness in subsequent arbitration or litigation proceedings and also protect his or her work product from being subpoenaed.

As a consequence of evidentiary rules and statutory privileges, information presented during a mediation is generally held in confidence by all participants and cannot be deemed discoverable during litigation. However, information that is otherwise admissible or discoverable is not protected merely because of its presentation during mediation. Depending on the jurisdiction, there are also several important exceptions to the confidential nature of mediation, including the legal requirement to disclose certain information, such as the revelation of plans to commit a crime.

In order to further safeguard the confidentiality of the proceedings, counsel should expressly agree that all statements made in the mediation are for the purpose of exploring the potential for compromise. Parties are also well advised to enter into contractual agreements which may include the destruction of the mediator's notes at the conclusion of the mediation and which may provide additional protections such as prohibiting public disclosure of the terms of any settlement agreement. Many mediators will include a provision on confidentiality and provide these additional protections in the mediator's agreement with the parties setting forth the terms of his or her engagement. (*See* Appendix G Bickerman Dispute Resolution Group Mediation Agreement). Additionally, where the parties are using an ADR provider, the organization will have procedural rules which address the issue of confidentiality.

While the concern for confidentiality is a legitimate one, parties to a dispute need to be practical and to recognize that mediation provides a higher level of confidentiality than the most likely alternative – unassisted negotiations between the parties.

## §6.10    PREPARE DRAFT SETTLEMENT AGREEMENT

Most mediation advocates give little thought, in advance of mediation, to the issues that need to be addressed in the event of a settlement. Preparing a draft of a binding term sheet, in advance of mediation, will save valuable time and assure counsel that all key settlement issues will be addressed before the parties adjourn. The exercise of drafting will require the consideration of the usual settlement issues such as releases, confidentiality, non-disparagement and termination of any pending litigation. This exercise will also permit counsel to create a checklist of any specific issues that need to be addressed in a settlement agreement. Counsel should also consider the advisability of arbitrating any future disputes that may arise between the parties.

# CHAPTER 7

## REPRESENTING THE CLIENT IN THE MEDIATION

## §7.1    COUNSEL'S ROLES IN MEDIATION SESSIONS

Once the mediation session begins, counsel has a continuing role as advocate, negotiator, counselor and problem-solver. Because a mediator often will involve the representatives of a party directly from the outset of the mediation session, some attorneys assume a passive role and are almost non-participants in the process. At the other extreme, some attorneys argue their clients' positions relentlessly and fail to advance their clients' interests by failing to take a more collaborative approach to the negotiations or permitting the client representative to be actively involved in the process.

Throughout the mediation, counsel should continue to pursue with the client the negotiating strategy adopted at the preparation stage. Counsel should remain an advocate in constant pursuit of the client's interests and goals. At the same time, counsel should listen carefully to the mediator, the opposing party and opposing counsel. The mediation sessions offer a time to learn more about the other party's case and an opportunity to reevaluate the client's goals and strategies. These sessions also offer a meaningful opportunity to solve the client's problem and accomplish its objectives.

## §7.2    OPENING STATEMENT

An opening statement in a joint session is an opportunity for the client to tell its story. Whether the story is presented by counsel or a representative of the client, the presenter should focus upon what a court will hear, not what happened. Recognizing that the mediation session will move from a form of mini-trial to a pure negotiation, counsel should lay a foundation for the negotiating positions the client ultimately will pursue. While it is appropriate to show anger or other feelings about the dispute, an opening statement should not use emotionally charged words which might simply antagonize the other side. To maximize the likelihood of success in mediation, counsel should demonstrate confidence in its position and, at the same time, indicate a willingness to engage in a good faith exploration of possible resolution. Finally, counsel and representatives of the parties should direct their comments to the other side, not to the mediator.

## §7.3    USE MEDIATOR TO FACILITATE NEGOTIATIONS

Counsel should recognize the competing tensions which exist in the relationship between counsel and the mediator. In a mediation, the parties are not only negotiating with each other, but the parties and counsel are also engaged in a mini-negotiation with the mediator, at least at the outset of the process. At the same time, by trusting the mediator with sensitive information about resolution, the parties are likely to enhance the potential for a successful resolution. Parties and counsel should also not hesitate to ask the mediator for needed information, make suggestions regarding process, ask the mediator to present a proposal as his or her own in order to overcome "reactive devaluation," or ask the mediator for substantive suggestions on settlement.

# §7.4     KEYS TO EFFECTIVE NEGOTIATIONS

As described in §1.3, the process of mediation is one of "facilitated negotiations." Success in mediation, therefore, very much depends upon the negotiating skill of the participants.  On the whole, even highly experienced lawyers and business executives approach negotiations on somewhat of an intuitive basis.  Yet, studies on negotiations establish that negotiation skills can be learned and that the skilled negotiat
or will outperform the average negotiator by substantial margins.  While the process of negotiations is itself the subject of numerous books and articles, the following sections offer some of the principal keys to successful negotiations in a mediation setting.

## §7.4.1     Ask Questions

Studies on negotiation demonstrate that skilled negotiators spend more than twice as much time gathering information as a percentage of their negotiating behavior as do average negotiators.  By asking questions, testing for understanding and summarizing, the skilled negotiator is in a far better position to understand the other side's interests, issues, perceptions and settlement positions.

## §7.4.2     Listen Carefully

Information is power.  A skilled negotiator will listen to every word to learn more about the other side's positions, perceptions and interests and to discern signals that may reveal the other side's settlement position.  For example, the statement "We're not prepared to make a significant move" should generate the responsive question "What do you regard as *significant*?" or "What move *are* you prepared to make?"  All too frequently, counsel will lose an opportunity to advance the negotiations by missing the subtle cues that can be learned from the spoken words, tone and non-verbal conduct of the participants in a negotiation.  While we all know how to listen, it is critical in a negotiation to filter out all the internal voices that may distract us from our full attention such as preparing a response to what is being said.

### §7.4.3      Develop Negotiating Power

Only two years after co-authoring *Getting to Yes: Negotiating Agreement Without Giving In* (Roger Fisher and William Ury, Houghton Mifflin Co., 1981), Roger Fisher recognized that this seminal work on using mediation to develop "win-win" solutions devoted insufficient attention to the issue of power. In "Negotiating Power" (*American Behavioral Scientist*, Vol. 27, No. 2, November/December 1983 149-166), Fisher explored the potential for successful negotiations as the result of recognizing and developing the sources of "real negotiating power." While it is a common misperception that real power arises from raw power or a tough approach to negotiations, Fisher described the following six kinds of power that, when properly understood and utilized, have a substantial ability to influence the outcome of a negotiation.

- *The power of skill and knowledge.* As suggested above, negotiating skills can be learned and a skilled negotiator can out-perform the average negotiator by substantial margins. Moreover, the more information a party learns about the facts, the rights, the interests and the people involved, the greater one's negotiating position.

- *The power of a good relationship.* A person's capacity to exert influence is substantially enhanced if he or she has established a well-deserved reputation for candor and integrity. Given the fact that the process of negotiations is one of communication, the process will be significantly enhanced by a good relationship with the other side. Not only will the other side listen better to messages delivered, but they will be more likely to be open when giving messages in response. These messages may well include signals that reveal the other side's settlement position.

- *The power of a good alternative to negotiation.* Power in negotiation very much depends upon how well a party will do in the event negotiations fail. For example, a customer complaining that a supplier has breached a supply agreement by failing to make timely deliveries will have substantial bargaining power if it can develop a readily available second source should the negotiations fail.

- *The power of an elegant solution.* The likelihood of success in negotiations can be enhanced by developing as many options as possible, especially a creative option that works well for both parties.

- *The power of legitimacy (fairness).* A party's negotiating power can be substantially enhanced by developing a set of standards (legal precedent, industry standards or policy considerations) that demonstrate the legitimacy (or fairness) of any proposal made to the other side.

- *The power of commitment.* A skilled negotiator will formulate an offer in ways that maximize the cumulative impact of each of the above sources of power. If an affirmative commitment to such an offer is rejected, a negative commitment (a threat or statement that no agreement is acceptable), may possibly undermine the potential for a successful result. As a consequence, it is generally unwise to make any such negative commitment until one has made the most of all of the other elements of negotiating power.

### §7.4.4    Understand Principles of Leverage

While one party in negotiations may have greater power in absolute (or objective) terms, the advantages of leverage can be determined by inquiring whether one of the parties to a dispute has a situational advantage. In many instances, the party with less power may have greater leverage. For example, a patent infringement claim by an inventor against a Fortune 500 company might represent just another claim in normal times. However, the same claim might present a strategic problem for the company if it is about to be acquired. In such a circumstance, while the large company has greater power, the inventor might have significant leverage in any negotiation to resolve the dispute. Leverage can be assessed by determining, for example, which party controls the status quo, whether time is an advantage for either party or whether one party has a greater need for confidentiality.

### §7.4.5    Demands and Offers

Demands and offers generally will be regarded by an adverse party as falling into one of the zones illustrated by the following graph.

### **Zones of Demands and Offers**

| Insult | Credible | Claimant Reasonable | Credible | Insult |
|--------|----------|---------------------|----------|--------|
|        |          | Respondent          |          |        |

In deciding what initial offer to make, the negotiator should recognize that any offer considered an insult may not generate any response and may possibly disrupt the negotiation. Conversely, opening with too much may embolden the other side and make the bargaining process harder, not easier. Further, there is always the potential that too large a move may exceed the bottom line requirements of the other side.

By making the first credible offer, parties have an opportunity to anchor the negotiation and adjust the expectations of the other side. In making an offer at the extreme edge of the credible zone, parties should advance a rationale to support the offer or expressly suggest that the offer is negotiable.

Once the negotiations are under way, counsel and parties in a mediation should consider empowering the mediator to control the flow of the negotiations. After having met with all parties in caucus sessions, the mediator can offer suggestions on process, comment on proposed offers and demands, especially if the mediator considers a negotiating move to be too large or too small. Especially with regard to the pace of the negotiations, parties need to trust the mediator and recognize that it may be counterproductive to try to close too fast. Of course, while the mediator may be in the best position to offer suggestions to advance the process, the dispute belongs to the parties – not to the mediator. Ultimately, the parties must decide what proposals to make and whether or not an amicable resolution presents a more attractive alternative than the consequences of failing to settle.

### §7.4.6  Track the Negotiations

Counsel should chart the progress of the negotiations by keeping a record of each new offer, demand or proposal. After the first several moves in a negotiation, a pattern may emerge from the proportional moves made by the parties. By reviewing the movement of the parties and the remaining gap, counsel can better determine whether smaller or larger moves should be made to advance the negotiations and accomplish the goals of the client.

### §7.4.7  Use Demonstrative Aids

Selective use of charts, exhibits and other visual aids can be very persuasive in mediation. In a joint session, an exhibit illustrating a design defect or a chart offering an accounting of probable damages can offer the other side a glimpse of what a jury is likely to see at trial. Moreover, unlike at trial, where an exhibit is marked and shown to the jury for a limited period of time, a visual aid can make a meaningful impact by remaining in the mediation room for an extended period of time. To the extent correspondence, memos or other documents are available to contradict positions likely to be taken by the adverse party, they should be available in mediation to be shared with the mediator.

## §7.5  ENCOURAGE CLIENT PARTICIPATION

Most mediation advocates are litigators who, as a consequence of their training and experience, often find it difficult to cede control of the process to the client. Once again, it is important to stress that the client needs to tell its story and have its "day in court." More importantly, business executives have the best understanding of the company's interests and objectives and are often in a better position than counsel to suggest or accept business-driven solutions to a dispute.

## §7.6    SOLVE THE PROBLEM

By taking a problem-solving approach to a dispute, counsel and the parties have the potential to create solutions that work for both parties. Much has been written about the potential for "win-win" solutions. While the potential is very real, it requires the participant in a negotiation to think "out of the box" – to continually brainstorm for creative solutions in meetings between counsel and the client, in joint sessions with the other sides, and in caucus sessions with the mediator. The downtime that occurs when a mediator is meeting with other parties in caucus sessions presents a particularly good time for party representatives to engage in such a brainstorming exercise. Counsel can enhance the potential for a creative solution by mining the depths of the parties' interests and by taking a collaborative approach to the negotiations. Ultimately, the parties may identify new opportunities such as, for example, amending the terms of a contract unrelated to the dispute or acquiring some or all of the assets (or shares) of the other party. For a thorough analysis of a problem-solving approach to negotiations and the potential rewards of such an approach, see Menkel-Meadow, Carrie, *Toward Another View of Legal Negotiation: The Structure of Problem Solving*, 31 UCLA Law Review 754 (1984).

## §7.7    COUNSEL'S ROLE AT END OF MEDIATION SESSIONS

Whether or not the mediation sessions produce an agreement, counsel should be mindful of his or her continuing role as counselor and advocate. Any settlement should be memorialized in a binding term sheet and signed by the parties to avoid any possible remorse by one of the parties or any later disagreement concerning the terms of settlement. If there is an agreement, counsel should make certain that any written agreement provides full protection for all of the client's concerns. If an agreement is not reached, counsel should immediately meet with the client to explore alternative negotiation and litigation strategies. If the client's interests are likely to be enhanced by the mediator's continuing involvement, counsel may want to initiate and help structure the mediator's continuing role.

## §7.8　ETHICAL STANDARDS FOR LAWYERS IN MEDIATION

The rules of professional conduct generally will govern a lawyer's conduct in a mediation setting. Most states have enacted codes which follow the ABA Model Rules of Professional Conduct. Since a mediation is primarily a negotiation, a lawyer will be expected in a mediation to adhere to the same standards as in an unassisted negotiation. The most important ethical rules are those governing advocacy, truthfulness, confidentiality and advice to the client. In particular, a lawyer has a duty to keep a client reasonably informed about the status of a matter and to promptly reply to reasonable requests for information from the client. This duty would require a lawyer, among other things, to advise a client about any settlement offer made during the course of a mediation. Further, counsel should be mindful throughout the course of negotiations and in the mediation session of the requirements of Rule 4.1 of the ABA Model Rules of Professional Conduct concerning "Truthfulness in Statements to Others." Rule 4.1, among other things, states that counsel shall not, in the course of representing a client, knowingly make a false statement of material fact or law to a third person.

## §7.9　10 PRACTICE TIPS FOR JOINT SESSIONS

Below is a summary of major points for the advocates in mediation joint sessions:

1. Confirm participation in good faith.

2. Use opening statements to tell client's story, educate the mediator, and persuade the other side.

3. Discuss what a court will hear, not what happened.

4. Direct communications to other side, not the mediator.

5.   Consider client participation.

6.   Help mediator clarify disputed issues.

7.   Permit venting, but do not antagonize.

8.   Do not review history of prior negotiations.

9.   Use visual aids.

10.  Listen actively and ask questions.

# §7.10   10 PRACTICE TIPS FOR CAUCUS SESSIONS

Below is a summary of major points for the advocate in mediation caucus sessions:

1.   Confirm mediator's pledge of confidentiality.

2.   Encourage client participation.

3.   Make proposals to generate movement.

4.   Use mediator to convey proposals.

5.   Ask for mediator to recommend substantive proposals.

6.   Make process suggestions to mediator.

7.   Track (chart) all negotiating positions during mediation.

8.  When mediator meets other side, use time to reevaluate positions and to brainstorm.

9.  Listen actively; information is power.

10.  Be patient; the process takes time.

## §7.11   25 PRACTICE TIPS FOR EFFECTIVE MEDIATION ADVOCACY

The following practice tips are offered to assist counsel with their preparation for a mediation:

1.  Before selecting a mediator, carefully examine the mediator's reputation, expertise, personality, style and experience.

2.  Interview mediator candidates to assess their experience, style and qualifications.

3.  Participate in the design of the mediation process.

4.  Be certain that all necessary parties and decision makers will be present during the mediation.

5.  Make sure that representatives of adverse parties have comparable settlement authority.

6.  Set aside sufficient time for the process.

7.  Before the mediation, perform a cost-benefit and litigation risk analysis.

8.  Avoid irrational attachments to positions.

9.  Review with your client its interests, goals, objectives and business needs. Prioritize the needs of your client and the opposing party.

10. Develop your client's "BATNA" (best alternative to a negotiated settlement) and "WATNA" (worst alternative to a negotiated settlement).

11. Educate your client about the mediation process, and explain the roles of the mediator, the advocate and the client.

12. Prepare for persuasive negotiations, not litigation.

13. Assess your client's ability to be articulate and determine, in advance, the most effective level of client participation.

14. Prepare client representatives for the likelihood that a mediator will ask questions such as "How do you feel about the dispute?" and "What is most important to you?"

15. Develop a specific negotiating strategy for the mediation. Continually reassess your strategy and revise it, as appropriate.

16. Present a concise opening statement that includes a factual summary and outline of the relevant issues and the strengths of your client's legal positions.

17. Direct your opening statements and argument to the opposing parties, not to counsel or the mediator.

18. Avoid the use of emotionally-charged language. Where appropriate, express empathy for the other parties' concerns.

19. Listen carefully. Parties are more open in a mediation session than in unassisted negotiations. Be on the lookout for signals from opposing parties throughout the mediation process.

20. Prepare, in advance, a few good reasons why the other party should move toward your settlement proposal.

21. Develop creative proposals that take into account underlying business interests and relationships between the parties.

22. Ask the mediator, where appropriate, to present settlement options as his or her own idea in order to avoid reactive devaluation.

23. Decide, in advance, what steps you and your client will take if mediation fails to achieve a negotiated settlement.

24. Anticipate the measures likely to be taken by adverse parties if the dispute is not resolved.

25. Remember that a "failed" mediation may be the catalyst for a subsequent negotiated resolution of the dispute.

# CHAPTER 8

## CASE STUDIES IN MEDIATION

§8.1    Major Bank v. High Tech Computer Corporation
§8.2    Insolvent Bank v. Law Firm
§8.3    Accounting Firm v. Departing Partners
§8.4    Shareholder Dispute among Family Members
§8.5    Defense Contractor v. Supplier


The following case studies offer concrete examples of why mediation is becoming more attractive as a dispute resolution alternative.


## §8.1    MAJOR BANK v. HIGH TECH COMPUTER CORPORATION

A high tech company entered into a contract with a major bank to provide a new software program designed to revolutionize accounting systems within the bank's trust department and to make the department far more profitable. After the high tech company failed several times to meet projected delivery schedules, the bank filed a lawsuit for breach of contract, seeking recovery of all monies paid and other consequential damages.

Before proceeding with lengthy and costly discovery, the parties agreed to devote one day to mediation. The mediator began by asking both parties to argue the "merits" of their respective positions. The presidents of both companies and their counsel attended the joint session. In the first caucus session with the bank, the mediator learned that the bank had not lost confidence in the software company's ultimate ability to provide the product consistent with the bank's needs and specifications. However, the bank had serious concerns about the software company's ability to meet its deadlines.

In the first caucus session with the software company, the mediator learned that the company needed time to work out problems within the system; that it was confident about its ability to perform in a timely manner; and that other banks were lined up to purchase the system if it worked as advertised. The mediator learned further that the potentially lucrative future of the company depended upon the successful completion of this first installation.

Over a two-day period (notwithstanding the initial agreement to mediate for only a day), the mediator was able to work directly with the parties to restructure their relationship. The software company was given additional time to complete the contract. Additionally, the terms between the parties were changed to give the bank (1) a slightly lower price for the software and (2) an interest in the software company's profits from future installations over a period of years.

## §8.2    INSOLVENT BANK v. LAW FIRM

A receiver was appointed by the court to govern the liquidation of an insolvent bank. Shortly after his appointment, the receiver reviewed the affairs of the bank for the decade preceding his appointment. He concluded that the insolvency would not have occurred but for the conduct of the law firm which had served as principal counsel to the bank.

The receiver filed a malpractice suit in the United States District Court laying the blame for the demise of the bank at the doorstep of the law firm. More specifically, the complaint alleged that a partner of the law firm who served on the bank's Board of Directors failed to uncover mismanagement and self-dealing on the part of the bank's principal officers. Adopting a "hear no evil, see no evil" approach to service on the board, the partner's inaction allegedly permitted management to remain entrenched and thus permitted the "looting" to continue. Throughout the decade, the law firm earned millions of dollars in fees for its legal services to the bank. The complaint alleged that the law firm's conduct constituted a conflict of interest, breach of contract, fraud and breach of fiduciary duties.

After four years of multiple motions and scores of depositions, the presiding judge ordered the parties to participate in private mediation. At the inception of the mediation, the plaintiff demanded "tens of millions" of dollars. Because the defendants regarded the lawsuit as wholly without merit, this demand was met with the response of "not a penny."

After permitting the parties to argue the merits of their positions for a few hours, the mediator challenged both parties in private caucuses to make a more realistic assessment of their case. The mediator spent hours with the parties exploring the weaknesses of their respective cases and assessing the likely risks and costs at trial. After this process, the mediator challenged plaintiff to lower its demand and defendants to make a credible offer. The mediator urged both parties to send the first signal, explaining the negotiating theory which suggests that the party making the "first credible move" can achieve a significant benefit.

Later that day, after almost eight hours of meeting in joint and caucus sessions, the defendants finally made an offer of more than "nuisance value." In response, plaintiff lowered its demand by a small amount. Defendants were persuaded to increase their offer even though they did so by only a small amount. The mediator then maintained the momentum by persuading the parties to make a significant number of small moves. Late in the evening, as a result of this signaling process, the dispute was settled in what is called a "tit for tat" negotiation.

In sum, the "case which could not be settled" was resolved because the mediator (1) challenged both sides in caucus sessions to recognize their weaknesses and reassess their positions, (2) persevered even when the parties viewed the situation as hopeless, and (3) offered the parties assistance with their negotiating strategies. Even in a difficult "pure dollars" dispute such as this one, the mediator was able to establish a level of communication which the parties had been unable to achieve on their own. As a consequence of the mediator's patience, determination and continued optimism, the parties remained together for over twelve hours. In an unassisted negotiation, it is likely that one of the parties would have abandoned the process.

## §8.3    ACCOUNTING FIRM v. DEPARTING PARTNERS

An accounting firm was experiencing significant difficulties among its partners over important strategic issues. After some debate within the partnership, the partners decided to remain together and seek the professional services of a consulting firm to consider the continued viability of the firm. Within several weeks, several partners abruptly left to establish their own competing firm.

The breakup of the accounting practice resulted in numerous charges and counter-charges from both groups over issues such as (1) entitlement to profits; (2) responsibility for debts; and (3) control of client accounts. In addition, the accounting firm charged the departing partners with breaching their fiduciary duties by allegedly "parking" opportunities and writing off time.

Both groups retained attorneys and threatened to sue for various claims. The parties, however, agreed to try mediation first. A mediator was able to overcome the emotional hostilities and get beyond the legal posturing by impressing upon all parties the need to resolve the dispute promptly, confidentially and in the interests of the clients of all parties. The mediator was able to resolve not only the monetary issues but also was able to seek agreement on many additional issues likely to arise, including some of the boundaries of future competition.

## §8.4    SHAREHOLDER DISPUTE AMONG FAMILY MEMBERS

A substantial family business was owned by four brothers and sisters who had inherited their interests from their father. Each of the four owned 25% of the shares in the company.

For over five years, the oldest brother had served as President and CEO of the company. During this period, although the value of the business continually declined, the President's salary and travel and entertainment budget increased. The siblings who were not actively involved in the business questioned whether their brother's level of income was warranted given the company's financial picture. However, they were unwilling to make any formal challenge because of their concern that their brother, the only one who knew how to run the business, would quit.

When the business continued to deteriorate, one of the brothers challenged his oldest brother and threatened legal action. Because of this challenge, the two brothers stopped talking to each other. An accountant who had served the company for two generations suggested voluntary mediation. All parties agreed.

A mediator was able to recognize that long-standing jealousies and other family issues played as large a role in the dispute as the business and legal issues. After allowing all of the parties to express their feelings and state their positions, the mediator then suggested a number of proposals. In the latter part of the session, an apology from the oldest brother for being too "high handed" in his management style went a long way toward bringing the parties together. Ultimately, all four agreed to resolve their dispute by selling the business and dividing the net proceeds.

## §8.5    DEFENSE CONTRACTOR v. SUPPLIER

Two large, multi-national corporations, embroiled in costly litigation for over two years, turned to mediation as an alternative. The litigation was commenced when a defense contractor sued a supplier for breach of contract alleging the supplier's failure to meet its deadlines under the contract. As a consequence, the contractor was forced to obtain the necessary component parts from a second source at a much higher price. The complaint sought damages for the difference in price.

The supplier contended that errors in the contractor's performance specifications made performance within the contract's stated deadlines an impossibility. The supplier filed a counterclaim for its payments due under the contract.

Approximately six months prior to trial, the presiding judge scheduled a pretrial conference to resolve the outstanding pretrial issues and to explore settlement. Counsel for both parties were instructed to discuss settlement with their respective clients prior to the court conference. Upon being approached by outside counsel, general counsel for the plaintiff expressed her concern over mounting legal fees and expenses. She further expressed the concern of the company's chief executive officer that the dispute was preventing discussion of other joint ventures with the supplier elsewhere in the world. Outside counsel for the contractor was instructed by the general counsel to suggest voluntary mediation to counsel for the supplier.

The general counsel noted that both corporations had signed the ADR pledge of the CPR Institute for Dispute Resolution, requiring the consideration of alternatives to litigation, where appropriate. She specifically suggested to outside counsel that this pledge, signed before the dispute arose, be mentioned to opposing counsel.

The supplier agreed to participate in the suggested mediation. In the initial joint session, both parties argued the merits of their respective legal positions. However, in private caucus sessions, both parties quickly conceded their desire to compromise the dispute. This concession was driven on both sides by (1) increasing fees and costs and (2) the recognition that the parties were unlikely to be able to pursue future joint ventures if the litigation continued and the level of trust between the parties continued to deteriorate.

Although outside counsel and high-level inside corporate counsel attended the mediation, the mediator was unable to resolve the dispute at the mediation session. He was unable to give the parties the one ingredient they both needed— time. Both sides needed more time to reevaluate their settlement positions. However, several weeks later, the parties decided that the chief executives of both companies should meet to continue the settlement negotiations. The dispute was resolved at this meeting, primarily because of the foundation provided by the voluntary mediation.

# CHAPTER 9

## CORPORATE AND LAW FIRM ADR STRATEGIES

## §9.1    INTRODUCTION

In the past several years, many corporations have reacted to the significant risks and costs of resolving disputes, and have begun implementing conflict management strategies and programs designed to resolve conflicts at the earliest stage possible. On the whole, law firms have responded less enthusiastically to the challenges and opportunities presented by the demands of their clients. A firm-wide ADR culture remains the exception. The law firm that assumes a leadership role on these issues, however, will have a significant advantage in the legal marketplace as we begin the 21st century.

## §9.2 CORPORATE ADR STRATEGIES

The elements of a corporate dispute resolution program can vary significantly, depending upon the objectives and culture of a particular corporation. There are certain elements and practices that are likely to enhance the success of any such program. The following "best practices" in ADR are offered as a guide to corporations desiring to make such a commitment.[1]

### § 9.2.1 Secure the Buy-in of Management

For a corporate ADR program to be successful, key executives in a company need to understand the economic benefits of an ADR approach to dispute resolution. Absent such an understanding, many executives initially take a win-at-any-cost approach until they begin to appreciate the substantial risks and costs of litigation. Executives should be made aware of the particular advantages of ADR including the potential for early disposition of disputes, the substantial savings in litigation costs, the desirability of avoiding the distractions of litigation, the benefits of privacy and confidentiality and, perhaps most importantly, the potential for business solutions that will serve the bottom-line interests of the company.

### §9.2.2 Commit Resources for ADR Education and Training

An up-front investment of time and money is necessary for an ADR program to succeed. In order for the law department and key executives to understand the benefits of ADR, training programs should be offered to enable these persons to understand the full range of options available to avoid, manage and resolve disputes. Companies should also make available books, periodicals, treatises, model policies and forms in order for key personnel to understand the important ADR issues and take a sophisticated approach in commercial transactions. Organizations such as the CPR Institute for Dispute Resolution, the American Arbitration Association, JAMS and the American Bar Association can

---

[1] Section 9.2 on "best practices" in corporate ADR is adapted from Chapter 57, "Alternative Dispute Resolution" of the multi-volume series entitled *Successful Partnering Between Inside and Outside Counsel*, authored by Jack L. Foltz and Bennett G. Picker, (Robert I. Haig, ed.) (West Group and ACCA 2000).

either provide or recommend highly qualified persons to conduct training programs.

### §9.2.3    Establish an In-house Advocate for ADR

The company should designate one person as the in-house advocate for ADR. Although this person may have other responsibilities, he or she can be responsible for establishing systems to avoid disputes, establishing policies for a sophisticated approach to commercial agreements, incorporating ADR into the company's policies for retention of outside counsel and designing programs for early case assessment. The ADR advocate should try to motivate people across departmental lines and encourage the establishment of ADR policies and practices that will serve the best interests of the company. Without a designated person to develop an organized approach to ADR, it will be difficult to overcome traditional preferences for litigation and the company's program will be less likely to succeed.

### §9.2.4    Insist that Outside Counsel Address ADR

Companies should insist that their outside law firms sign the CPR pledge on ADR which states

> "We recognize that for many disputes there may be methods more effective for resolution than traditional litigation. Alternative dispute resolution (ADR) procedures – used in conjunction with litigation or independently – can significantly reduce the cost and burdens of litigation and result in solutions not available in court. In recognition of the foregoing, we subscribe to the following statements of policy on behalf of our firm. First, appropriate lawyers in our firm will be knowledgeable about ADR. Second, where appropriate, the responsible attorney will discuss with the client the availability of ADR procedures so the client can make an informed choice concerning resolution of the dispute."

To date, over 1,500 law firms have signed this pledge.

In addition, companies should ask their outside law firms what measures they have undertaken to make this pledge a reality. More specifically, they should ask what formal training has been provided to the firm and whether there is an ADR practice group or individuals within the firm to serve as advisors at more sophisticated levels both to the client and to other firm members.

At a very minimum, a company should insist in its retention letter that outside counsel recommend ADR options, where appropriate. Additionally, many companies have adopted early case evaluation protocols which require their outside law firms, at an early stage of every dispute, to provide a written assessment of the risks and costs of litigation and any recommended ADR strategies. Some companies have adopted formal policies requiring their outside law firms within ninety days of the making of a claim or the filing of litigation to make an assessment of why a case is inappropriate for ADR before permitting a case to continue in litigation.

### §9.2.5    Establish a Suitability Screen to Determine Whether the Case is Appropriate for ADR

Companies should develop a "suitability screen" to assist in determining whether a case is appropriate for mediation or some other non-traditional ADR alternative. Suitability screens have been adopted by the CPR Institute for Dispute Resolution, a number of companies and law firms. (*See* Appendix C, Stradley, Ronon, Stevens & Young ADR Suitability Screen). These screens provide checklists to permit lawyers to determine whether a business dispute is suitable for resolution through ADR. The screens ask questions relating to the parties to the dispute, the role of counsel, the interests the parties are advancing and the outcomes the parties are seeking. Examples of such questions include the following:

- Are parties members of the CPR Institute for Dispute Resolution or other industry-based ADR pact?

- Would a presentation by one party's counsel to the other side promote a more realistic case assessment?

- Is confidentiality important?

- Do the parties seek a resolution that a court could not order?

## §9.2.6    Incorporate Multi-Tiered ADR Provisions in Contracts

Many companies historically have inserted a boilerplate arbitration clause in commercial agreements to provide an alternative to litigation.  Companies should take a far more sophisticated approach and, depending upon the transaction, should consider a multi-tiered approach calling for neutral fact-finding, executive negotiations and mediation as a predicate to either arbitration or litigation.  Dispute resolution clauses in commercial agreements are not "one size fits all."  The kind of dispute likely to arise should dictate the preferred dispute resolution option in a commercial agreement, as illustrated by the following examples:

- Will the client want a quick, negotiated resolution? (Mediation)

- Is there a non-negotiable interest which needs protection? (Litigation)

- Will there likely be a large volume of small dollar disputes? (Arbitration)

- Will there be a small number of big dollar disputes? (Mediation)

- Is the transaction a cross-border one? (Arbitration)

Dispute resolution clauses should be inserted in early drafts of agreements where they can be given the full attention they deserve.  In drafting dispute resolution clauses, a company should create a checklist that reflects its particular business concerns and focuses upon the key legal issues.

### §9.2.7    Use Negotiation and Mediation as Tools to Resolve Disputes

In focusing upon ADR, companies should not overlook the possibility of direct and unassisted negotiations as the initial path to resolution of a dispute. Any dispute appropriate for a negotiated resolution is also appropriate for mediation. Mediation should be considered, wherever possible, as a powerful tool to resolve disputes early, cost-effectively and fairly. Mediators can focus on the underlying business interests of the parties and attempt to fashion solutions that advance both sets of interests, rather than merely vindicating the rights of one party. In many situations, a skilled mediator can overcome the barriers that have arisen in an unassisted negotiation and facilitate creative, business-driven solutions that are simply unavailable in the win-lose environment of litigation.

### §9.2.8    Encourage Adversaries to Use ADR

Any company that has made a major internal commitment to adopt an ADR approach to dispute resolution should have, as one of its goals, motivating its adversaries to use ADR. Some companies are reluctant to suggest ADR or mediation to an adversary for fear of showing weakness and losing leverage in negotiations. Properly presented, however, this should not be a major concern. At the appropriate juncture in a dispute, a company can suggest mediation by stating "We're so sure a mediator will validate the strength of our position that we're willing to take the risk we are wrong." If the adversary is reluctant because of its unfamiliarity with ADR or mediation, neutral organizations such as the CPR Institute for Dispute Resolution have a good track record of convincing parties of the benefits of ADR. Where adversaries have signed the CPR pledge to use ADR or a similar pledge in an industry treaty, parties can be reminded of these commitments made prior to the existence of a dispute. Since mediation is non-binding, parties can consider giving the adversary a fair degree of control over decisions such as the designation of the neutral or the recommendation of procedures.

### §9.2.9    Litigate When Necessary

When there is the need to defend a frivolous case, to file an injunction, to establish a precedent or to protect a strategic interest, litigation may well be the best option.  Discovery and motion practice remain important tools in litigation.  There is simply no substitute for good case preparation and strong trial skills.  Moreover, a readiness to litigate when appropriate will permit a party to negotiate in an ADR setting from a position of strength.  The initial decision to litigate, however, should be reviewed at every critical stage of the litigation process.  Even after litigation has commenced, mediation may still offer the most direct and least costly path toward a favorable result.

### §9.2.10    Be Patient. Track and Measure the Results

Once a company places well-drawn ADR provisions in its commercial agreements and employment manual, some time may elapse before a dispute arises that is covered by the new language.  Therefore, it may be some time before a company can determine whether it is in a position to achieve earlier and less expensive resolutions in a private manner.  Some companies have reported publicly that the widespread use of ADR techniques has resulted in the reduction of claims and proceedings (measured in the thousands) and savings of defense expenses and settlement payments (measured in the millions) each year.  Take the time to measure and record the results and to compare them to the cost and time associated with disputes resolved in litigation.  It takes time to build a successful program and not every ADR experience will be positive.  Over time, however, an ADR approach to dispute resolution should yield substantial benefits.

The CPR Institute for Dispute Resolution has also developed strategies and tactics to help companies resolve disputes in ways that reinforce business goals and relationships (*See* Cronin-Harris, Catherine, *Building ADR into the Corporate Law Department* (CPR Institute for Dispute Resolution, 1997)).  In each instance, companies need to formulate approaches consistent with their objectives and culture. The most effective results will come only if there is a systematic inclusion of ADR options in the conflict management process.

## §9.3     LAW FIRM ADR STRATEGIES

Over 1,500 law firms have signed the CPR Law Firm Statement on Alternatives to Litigation. This commitment requires firm lawyers to be knowledgeable about ADR and, where appropriate, discuss with the client the advisability of ADR procedures so the client can make a reasoned choice concerning the resolution of the dispute (*See* Appendix B-2).

In order to breathe life into this pledge, however, a law firm needs to make a meaningful commitment to provide ADR counseling and advocacy services at sophisticated levels. The CPR Institute for Dispute Resolution has developed a multi-step program for law firms seeking to systematically include ADR in the dispute management services offered to clients (*See* Cronin-Harris, Catherine, *Building ADR into the Law Firm* (CPR Institute for Dispute Resolution, 1997)). The following is an outline of this program:

- *ADR Structures and Policies*

    - organize an ADR planning committee and ADR department
    - appoint a senior partner as ADR counsel
    - adopt a law firm ADR policy statement

- *Tailored ADR Training and Resources*

    - address common ADR obstacles
    - enlist support of the firm's ADR practitioners
    - provide ADR training and resources
    - encourage ADR research

- *Systematic ADR Case Analysis*

    - develop suitability screens
    - promote use of ADR in contract clauses

- *Full Range of ADR Services*

  - educate clients and market the firm's ADR services
  - establish ADR billing policies
  - offer ADR advocacy, counseling and neutral services

- *ADR Advocacy Strategies*

  - probe client's interest in ADR
  - get parties to the negotiating table
  - tailor ADR processes to case needs
  - limit ADR discovery practice
  - select client representatives for ADR
  - prepare for mediation and arbitration sessions

- *ADR Tracking Practices*

  - develop closed-case routines
  - create tracking forms and catalogue the data

The above strategies are intended for larger firms desiring to promote a firm-wide culture that embraces an ADR approach to conflict management and dispute resolution. At the very least, every law firm should have an appreciation for the landscape of ADR and the advantages offered by mediating business disputes. Even in smaller firms, one or more lawyers can assume the responsibility for understanding the suitability, preparation and advocacy issues at sophisticated levels. Whatever the size of the firm, every lawyer engaged in resolving business disputes can achieve significant benefits for the client by systematically including mediation as a dispute resolution alternative in the appropriate case.

# CHAPTER 10

## THE FUTURE OF MEDIATION –
## NEW CHALLENGES AND OPPORTUNITIES

§10.1  INTRODUCTION
§10.2  THE CHANGING WORLD OF DISPUTE RESOLUTION
§10.3  NEW ROLES FOR THE LEGAL PROFESSION
§10.4  MY OWN CHANGING WORLD
§10.5  NEW CHALLENGES FOR THE LEGAL PROFESSION
§10.6  CONCLUSION:  THE REWARDS OF ADDING VALUE

## §10.1  INTRODUCTION

As I have suggested throughout this text, mediation has dramatically changed the landscape of dispute resolution over the past couple of decades.  As the result of (1) multistep dispute resolution provisions in contracts; (ii) state and federal court-mandated mediation programs; (iii) governmental agency programs requiring mediation; and, perhaps most significantly, (iv) corporate America's mandate to use mediation where appropriate, mediation is now part of the fabric of dispute resolution in the United States.  Recent developments in the United Kingdom and elsewhere suggest the potential for significant change worldwide.

This chapter explores the opportunities and challenges mediation presents for the entire legal profession.

## §10.2  THE CHANGING WORLD OF DISPUTE RESOLUTION

In the world of business disputes, our universe has changed rapidly in recent years.  While the adversarial system remains the model for establishing truth and rights, our clients' perspectives have shifted dramatically when it comes to business disputes.  In most business disputes, clients now seek solutions that focus as much upon the underlying interests as upon truth and rights.  Speed and cost are often the paramount concerns.

Those of us on the front line of dispute resolution can almost feel the velocity of change. Only several years ago, the suggestion to mediate a dispute often had to be coupled with an explanation of the process. Experienced lawyers frequently confused mediation with arbitration. Mediation now is becoming commonplace and is gaining momentum as an enormously powerful tool to resolve disputes early, cost-effectively and fairly.

## §10.3    NEW ROLES FOR THE LEGAL PROFESSION

Today, our lens upon the world of dispute resolution is much wider, our approaches far more strategic. Lawyers are spending far more time with their clients discussing their interests and objectives. Depending upon the client's needs, the path to resolution might be negotiation or litigation. It might also be arbitration, mediation or even a customized ADR process. In numerous ways, the changing landscape of dispute resolution has impacted the daily life of practicing lawyers.

In business agreements, lawyers are inserting dispute resolution clauses in early drafts, where they can be given the full attention they deserve. In more complex agreements, we frequently provide for a multi-tiered approach calling for neutral fact-finding, executive negotiations and mediation as a predicate to either arbitration or litigation.

For those disputes that do arise, many law firms and corporations have developed suitability screens to provide for a focused analysis of the most appropriate dispute resolution alternatives. We also regularly address questions such as "How do we propose mediation to a reluctant adversary?" or "Should we select a more facilitative or more evaluative mediator for this particular dispute?"

As advocates in ADR settings, lawyers recognize that preparing the case is quite different from preparing for litigation. In a mediation, for example, we invariably begin with a traditional rights analysis – an understanding of the legally cognizable claims and defenses. Equally important, however, is an understanding of the client's (and the adversary's) industries, their business operations and their objectives. In preparing for mediation, we need to prepare the client for questions that a witness almost never would be asked in a courtroom – questions such as

"How do you feel about this dispute?" or "What do you need the most?" Once in mediation, it is important to execute a well thought out, yet flexible, negotiating plan. Many attorneys do not fully understand the mediation process and do not prepare adequately. These attorneys lose enormous opportunities for their client.

Lawyers are also undertaking exciting new assignments which place a premium on creative lawyering. Lawyers are being engaged as "ADR process counsel" or "settlement counsel" to monitor ongoing litigation and develop early exit strategies. We are also developing employment ADR systems – designs for preventing disputes as much as resolving them. Permitting employees to air their grievances early so they do not become full-blown disputes, these programs often employ procedures such as independent investigation by ombudspersons and peer review and provide for mediation and arbitration as final steps.

## §10.4   MY OWN CHANGING WORLD

In my own firm, we have worked with corporate counsel to develop early case assessment programs and to provide ADR education and training. We have also participated actively in organizations such as the CPR Institute for Dispute Resolution, the American Arbitration Association, the American Bar Association and the American Corporate Counsel Association. I should add that we have had a great deal of fun in the process. Meeting regularly, our ADR Practice Group members compare notes, discuss cutting-edge ADR issues and publish a substantive, quarterly ADR newsletter. We have also conducted numerous educational programs and in-house client briefings on ADR. Our firm is only one of many with active ADR practices, giving new meaning to the concept of "partnering" with our clients.

After decades as a litigator, I am now spending most of my professional time as a mediator. In many respects, I have found serving as a mediator to be at least as demanding as trying a case. I am called upon to apply the skills of a litigator, a negotiator, an advocate, a counselor, a diplomat and a psychologist. Serving as a mediator has its own set of challenges, such as the need to recall after the sixth or seventh hour precisely what information is and is not confidential; the need to explore the depths of personal and business relationships; and the need for endless amounts of perseverance and optimism necessary to bring parties together. At the same time, the rewards are great. I can recall a mediation between two healthcare institutions where, in twenty straight hours, we resolved not only every disputed issue, but also unrelated issues ripe for future disagreement. My sense of personal accomplishment working with the parties was as great as in any major victory in litigation.

## §10.5   NEW CHALLENGES FOR THE LEGAL PROFESSION

For the entire legal profession, the new world of conflict management and dispute resolution provides both exciting new challenges and new opportunities. It also requires new approaches and new skills. For all of us, first and foremost, there is a need to change our traditional approach to resolving disputes, even a need to change our basic attitudes. We need to redefine the very meaning of what it is to "win". Consistent with what our clients want and deserve, the ultimate "win" requires our understanding of the client's needs and an ability to solve their problems.

For lawyers, this means new approaches that initially seem almost counter-intuitive. For example, the recovery of large sums of money is usually regarded as the ultimate "win" for plaintiffs in commercial cases. Yet, Wall Street values long-term streams of revenue even more highly than large sums of cash. Perhaps the restructuring of a long-term relationship would offer a better result. Once in mediation, lawyers usually try to exert a high degree of control over the process, not unlike in a deposition or at trial. However, direct involvement of the client in the mediation process is often the best way to succeed. Lawyers also frequently engage in a "we-they" approach to negotiations that rarely results in the creative solutions that can arise from a more collaborative approach. Lawyers need to have a better understanding of the importance of integrative bargaining, where lawyers can sit on the same side of the table and try to "expand the pie". They also need to reflect upon the meaning of Rule 1.3 of the ABA Model Rules of Professional Conduct, imposing a duty to represent a client zealously. Effective mediation advocates need to abandon any desire for revenge in favor of a more goal oriented approach if they are to secure the "win" that best serves their client's interests.

For law firms, there is a need to take the long-term view. Many law firms have been reluctant to embrace an ADR approach to dispute resolution. These firms see ADR as an incursion into a significant profit center. Professional responsibility aside, the world of ADR is here to stay and those who take a leadership position are likely to gain a significant competitive advantage. This is especially so given the rapid expansion of the accounting firms and multi-disciplinary practices into the world of dispute resolution.

For business clients, there is a need to manage disputes more effectively. To do so, clients need to depart from an *ad hoc* approach to dispute resolution. Clients need to secure the buy-in of management, make an up-front investment in training and resources, develop programs for early case assessment and ongoing management of disputes and establish systems to track and measure the results.

For law schools, there is a need to recognize that the demands of the marketplace have forever changed the dynamics of dispute resolution. Obviously, an understanding of the adversarial system, *stare decisis* and the process of litigation remains critical. At the same time, students need to enhance their skills as negotiators and to appreciate, for example, the value of listening and the advantage of making the "first credible offer." Law students also need to understand the suitability and advocacy issues in ADR at more sophisticated levels and to understand the important keys to problem-solving.

For the mediation and ADR community, we need to assure quality, especially at a time when so many lawyers without experience are trying their hand as neutrals. Even more experienced mediators need to enhance their skills by exchanging views with their colleagues on issues such as breaking impasse, mediation transparency, or power imbalance. There is also a need to define the rules for those serving as neutrals – an area that is mostly uncharted waters. Fortunately, there are some beacons of light to provide us with guidance in this brave new world of dispute resolution. Institutions such as the American Bar Association Section of Dispute Resolution, the American Arbitration Association, and the CPR Institute for Dispute Resolution are regularly grappling with the need for education, training and guidelines.

## §10.6    CONCLUSION:  THE REWARDS OF ADDING VALUE

While there are many new challenges, there are also new opportunities and new rewards.  The world of ADR, unbounded by strict rules of litigation, is limited only by one's imagination. Lawyers are designing new and imaginative approaches to dispute resolution every day.  The emerging field of "transformative mediation" in employment disputes, for example, strives not only to resolve the employee's grievance but also to enhance morale in the workplace. "Consensus building," another example, permits the design of a process to avoid escalating confrontations with governmental agencies and stakeholder groups.

For both corporate counsel and the private bar, the problem-solving approach to dispute resolution can be extraordinarily stimulating and rewarding. Each next case requires a fresh new approach, an understanding of the client's business and objectives and far more communication with the client. As we move forward in the 21$^{st}$ century, we can move beyond the "win-lose" environment of litigation to the full range of ADR options available to avoid disputes and solve our clients' problems.  By making this commitment to ADR, we have the opportunity to add substantial value both to our clients and to our profession.

# APPENDIX A

## SELECTED READINGS ON MEDIATION AND NEGOTIATION

## I. MEDIATION

Bush, Robert A. Baruch and Joseph P. Folger, *The Promise of Mediation* (Jossey-Bass Publishers, 1994)

Cooley, John W., *Mediation Advocacy* (National Institute for Trial Advocacy, 1996)

Fisher, Roger and William Ury, *Getting To Yes: Negotiating Agreement Without Giving In* (Houghton Mifflin Co., 1981)

Galton, Eric, *Representing Clients in Mediation* (Texas Lawyer Press, 1994)

Golann, Dwight, *Mediating Legal Disputes: Effective Strategies for Lawyers and Mediators* (Little, Brown and Company, 1996)

Goldberg, Stephen B., Eric D. Green, and Frank E.A. Sander, *Dispute Resolution* (Little, Brown and Company, 1985)

Henry, James F. and Jethro K. Lieberman, *The Manager's Guide to Resolving Legal Disputes* (Harper & Row, 1985)

Kovach, Kimberlee K., *Mediation: Principles and Practice* (West Publishing Co., 1994)

Moore, Christopher W., *The Mediation Process* (Jossey-Bass Publishers 1986)

Riskin, Leonard L., *The Contemplative Lawyer: On the Potential Contributions of Mindfulness of Mediation to Law Students, Lawyers and Their Clients* (7 Harvard Negotiation Law Review 1 2002)

Rogers, Nancy and Craig A. McEwen, *Mediation: Law, Policy, Practice* (Lawyer's Cooperative Publishing, 1989)

Williams, Gerald R., *Legal Negotiation and Settlement* (West Publishing Co., 1983)

Van Winkle, John R., *Mediation: A Path Back For the Lost Lawyer* (ABA Section of Dispute Resolution, 2001)

## II.  NEGOTIATION

Bazerman, Max H. and Margaret A. Neale, *Negotiating Rationally* (The Free Press, 1992)

Fisher, Roger, *Negotiating Power* (American Behavorial Scientist, Vol. 27, No. 2, November/December 1983)

Guthrie,Chris, Jeffrey J. Rachlinski & Andrew J. Winstrich, *Inside the Judicial Mind* (86 Cornell Law Review 4, May 2001)

Menkel-Meadow, Carrie, *Toward Another View of Legal Negotiation: The Structure of Problem Solving* (31 UCLA Law Review 754 1984)

Mnookin, Robert H., *Why Negotiations Fail: An Exploration of Barriers to Resolution of Conflict* (8 Ohio State Journal on Dispute Resolution 235, 1993)

Mnookin, Robert H., Scott R. Peppet, and Andrew S. Tulumello, *Beyond Winning: Negotiating to Create Value in Deals and Disputes* (Harvard University Press, 2000).

Shell, Richard G., *Bargaining For Advantage* (Viking Penguin, 1999)

Ury, William, *Getting Past No: Negotiating with Difficult People* (Bantam Books, 1991)

Williams, Gerald R., *Negotiation as a Healing Process,* (J. Disp. Res. 1, 1996)

## III. ETHICS

Bernard, Phyllis and Bryant Garth, *Dispute Resolution Ethics: A Comprehensive Guide* (ABA Section of Dispute Resolution, 2002)

## IV. GENERAL ADR

Alfini, James J. and Eric R. Galton, *ADR Personalities and Practice Tips* (ABA Section of Dispute Resolution, 1998)

# APPENDIX B

## CPR CORPORATE AND LAW FIRM STATEMENTS

## ON ALTERNATIVES TO LITIGATION

The CPR Institute for Dispute Resolution is a nonprofit initiative of 500 general counsel of major corporations, leading law firms and prominent legal academics in support of alternatives to litigation. CPR develops new methods to resolve business and public disputes by alternative dispute resolution (ADR).

## APPENDIX B-1

---

# CPR CORPORATE POLICY STATEMENT
## on
# ALTERNATIVES TO LITIGATION©

---

COMPANY

We recognize that for many disputes there is a less expensive, more effective method of resolution than the traditional lawsuit. Alternative dispute resolution (ADR) procedures involve collaborative techniques which can often spare businesses the high costs of litigation.

In recognition of the foregoing, we subscribe to the following statements of principle on behalf of our company and its domestic subsidiaries:[*]

In the event of a business dispute between our company and another company which has made or will then make a similar statement, we are prepared to explore with that other party resolution of the dispute through negotiation or ADR techniques before pursuing full-scale litigation. If either party believes that the dispute is not suitable for ADR techniques, or if such techniques do not produce results satisfactory to the disputants, either party may proceed with litigation.

---

CHIEF EXECUTIVE OFFICER

---

CHIEF LEGAL OFFICER

---

DATE

---

[*] Our major operating subsidiaries are:

---

**More than 4,000 operating companies have committed to the Corporate Policy Statement on Alternatives to Litigation**[©]. The CPR Corporate Pledge obliges subscribing companies to seriously explore negotiation, mediation or other ADR processes in conflicts arising with other signatories before pursuing full-scale litigation. The list of companies subscribing on behalf of themselves and their major operating subsidiaries is available on the CPR Web site (www.cpradr.org).

**CPR Institute for Dispute Resolution**
366 Madison Avenue, New York, NY 10017 : Tel (212) 949-8859 : Internet:www.cpradr.org

## APPENDIX B-2

# CPR LAW FIRM POLICY STATEMENT
## on
# ALTERNATIVES TO LITIGATION©

## FIRM

## ADDRESS

## CITY, STATE, ZIP

## TELEPHONE

We recognize that for many disputes there may be methods more effective for resolution than traditional litigation. Alternative dispute resolution (ADR) procedures—used in conjunction with litigation or independently—can significantly reduce the costs and burdens of litigation and result in solutions not available in court.

In recognition of the foregoing, we subscribe to the following statements of policy on behalf of our firm.

First, appropriate lawyers in our firm will be knowledgeable about ADR.

Second, where appropriate, the responsible attorney will discuss with the client the availability of ADR procedures so the client can make an informed choice concerning resolution of the dispute.

CHIEF EXECUTIVE OFFICER

CHIEF LEGAL OFFICER

DATE

**More than 1,500 law firms have signed the CPR Law Firm Policy Statement on Alternatives to Litigation©, including 400 of the nation's 500 largest firms.** The Law Firm Pledge obliges subscribing firms to assure that appropriate lawyers are knowledgeable about ADR and to discuss the availability of ADR with clients. The full list of subscribers is available on the CPR Web site (www.cpradr.org).

**CPR Institute for Dispute Resolution**
366 Madison Avenue, New York, NY 10017 : Tel (212) 949-8859 : Internet:www.cpradr.org

# APPENDIX C
## ADR SUITABILITY SCREEN[1]

  This ADR Suitability Screen is designed for use by firm lawyers in advising clients as to whether a business dispute is suitable for resolution through ADR. While a "yes" answer tends to support an ADR alternative and a "no" answer suggests the opposite, the Suitability Screen is intended to be predictive, not determinative. In addition, answers to some questions may carry more weight than others, in a particular case. Further, a "no" answer to certain questions, marked with an asterisk, may not necessarily argue against ADR. Finally, consideration should also be given to how the views of opposing counsel (and not just the opposing party) will affect suitability for resolution by ADR.

  The ADR Practice Group stands ready to assist firm lawyers in any evaluation.

|  |  | Yes | No |
|---|---|---|---|
| **I.** | **The Parties and Their Relationships** |  |  |
| 1. | The parties involved are signatories to the CPR pledge or an industry-based ADR pact, or are otherwise committed to exploring ADR alternatives. |  |  |
| 2. | Apart from the dispute, the actual or potential business relationships among the parties are significant, and are likely to stay that way. |  | * |
| 3. | The people with authority to resolve the dispute on both sides either are or can be involved in its resolution. |  |  |

---

[1]  The above ADR Suitability Screen was designed by the ADR Practice Group of Stradley Ronon Stevens & Young, LLP (Philadelphia, PA).

|  |  | Yes | No |
|---|---|---|---|
| 4. | The other side's view of its case has been colored by an unrealistic appraisal by its counsel; a direct approach to the other side will be helpful. |  |  |
| 5. | A presentation by counsel might promote a better understanding of the issues or a more realistic case assessment. |  |  |
| 6. | The parties' decision makers lack familiarity with the facts or merits of the dispute. |  |  |
| 7. | At least one side is genuinely interested in compromise. |  |  |
| 8. | At this point, the general attitude of each side toward the other is relatively objective. |  |  |
| 9. | A non-binding evaluation from a skilled neutral would help produce a more realistic assessment from either side. |  | * |
| 10. | A mediator or neutral facilitator would help diffuse hostility between lawyers or parties. |  |  |
| 11. | There are multiple parties involved, escalating the time and costs of litigation. |  | * |
| 12. | In terms of financial resources, business sophistication and litigation experience, the sides are substantially comparable. |  |  |
| **II.** | **Interests That the Parties Are Advancing** |  |  |
| 13. | The jurisdiction in which the dispute is pending requires some form of non-binding ADR in this type of case. |  |  |
| 14. | A speedy and inexpensive resolution of the dispute is important to both parties. |  |  |

|  |  | Yes | No |
|---|---|---|---|
| 15. | The parties want to avoid publicity. |  |  |
| 16. | The transaction costs of pursuing litigation, compared to what either side can realistically expect to recover or save, are disproportionately large. |  | * |
| 17. | Confidentiality is an important concern for at least one party. |  |  |
| 18. | The dispute presents risks for either side of damage to reputation, public rejection of a product, potentially greater governmental regulation or some comparable risk. |  | * |
| 19. | The parties want to reach a business solution rather than an outcome resulting in money damages only. |  |  |
| 20. | Both sides wish to avoid burdensome or intrusive full-blown discovery. |  |  |
| **III.** | **Issues Involved and Outcomes Sought** |  |  |
| 21. | The issues involved in the dispute are sensitive, involving senior management, disclosure of trade secrets or production of sensitive documents. |  | * |
| 22. | The issues involved in the dispute are highly technical or complex. |  | * |
| 23. | The central issues in this dispute are factual, but do not turn on the credibility of key witnesses. |  | * |
| 24. | One or more sides seeks a resolution that a court could not grant, such as a modification of the relationship between or among the parties. |  |  |

| | | Yes | No |
|---|---|---|---|
| 25. | Either side has something significant left to put on the table to induce settlement. | | |
| 26. | The parties wish to control the outcome of the dispute by avoiding binding adjudication and the attendant risk of loss. | | |
| 27. | Inflicting significant damage on the other side or securing public vindication is of no interest to either side. | | |
| 28. | The parties need a speedy resolution. | | * |
| 29. | The dispute is ripe for resolution. | | |
| 30. | There are business issues collateral to the dispute that may also be resolved. | | * |
| 31. | There is at least some merit to both sides; the claim is **not** frivolous. | | |
| 32. | A public victory will **not** deter future claims. | | |
| 33. | The dispute is one of a substantial number of pending or potential claims stemming from the same fact pattern or event, and a lower profile, confidential ADR process will reduce the incidence of claims. | | |
| 34. | There is no need for a decisive legal precedent. | | |
| 35. | There is no need for injunctive relief. | | |
| 36. | The likelihood that this case can be disposed of by a prompt dispositive motion is speculative. | | |
| 37. | The chances of winning at trial are unknown or uncertain. | | |

# APPENDIX D

## AAA COMMERCIAL MEDIATION RULES

*As Amended and Effective on July 1, 2002*

**AMERICAN ARBITRATION ASSOCIATION**

# INTRODUCTION

In some situations, the involvement of an impartial mediator can assist parties in reaching a settlement of a commercial dispute. Mediation is a process under which the parties submit their dispute to an impartial person—the mediator. The mediator may suggest ways of resolving the dispute, but may not impose a settlement on the parties.

If the parties want to use a mediator to resolve an existing dispute under these rules, they can enter into the following submission.

*The parties hereby submit the following dispute to mediation administered by the American Arbitration Association under its Commercial Mediation Rules (the clause may also provide for the qualifications of the mediator, the method of payment, the locale of meetings, and any other item of concern to the parties).*

If the parties want to adopt mediation as an integral part of their contractual dispute settlement procedure, they can insert the following mediation clause into their contract in conjunction with a standard arbitration provision.

*If a dispute arises out of or relates to this contract or the breach thereof and if the dispute cannot be settled through negotiation, the parties agree first to try in good faith to settle the dispute by mediation administered by the American Arbitration Association under its Commercial Mediation Rules before resorting to arbitration, litigation, or some other dispute resolution procedure.*

The American Arbitration Association is a public service, not-for-profit organization offering a broad range of dispute resolution services to business executives, attorneys, individuals, trade associations, unions, management, consumers, families, communities, and all levels of government. Services are available through offices located in major cities throughout the United States. Mediation conferences may be held at locations convenient for the parties and are not limited to cities with AAA offices. In addition, the AAA serves as a center for education and training, issues specialized publications, and conducts research on all forms of out-of-court dispute settlement.

# RESOLVING BUSINESS DISPUTES

Business disputes may be submitted to a special program of alternatives to litigation.

### How the Program Works

Any party to an existing business dispute may ask the AAA to ascertain willingness of the other party or parties to submit the dispute to alternative dispute resolution (ADR). Cases that are new or pending litigation are eligible.

An AAA representative will explain the various dispute resolution techniques and assist the parties in choosing one that meets their needs. Once the AAA has the parties' agreement to submit a dispute to alternative dispute resolution, it will administer the case under its applicable rules or procedures.

Beyond mediation, ADR might take the form of arbitration, mini-trial, or any variation of these procedures on which the parties agree.

*Arbitration* is the process in which each side presents its case at a hearing to a neutral or panel of arbitrators for a final and binding decision.

*Mini-trial* is a structured settlement procedure in which attorneys present their best case in an abbreviated form with experts, if appropriate, before senior executives of the companies involved and a neutral who chairs the presentation. After the presentation, the senior executives meet for a settlement discussion. In the event that the senior executives are unable to settle the dispute, the neutral may be empowered to mediate and/or provide a nonbinding advisory opinion regarding the likely outcome if the case were to be litigated.

*Advisory arbitration* in most respects mirrors traditional arbitration. It differs, however, in focusing on specific issues in a dispute and deciding them in an award that is not binding on the parties.

*Other ADR methods* include factfinding, investigation of a dispute by a neutral who issues findings and a nonbinding report, and med-arb, which combines the two primary processes.

## The Neutrals

Mediators and arbitrators selected for this program are qualified, experienced neutrals with an understanding of current legal and business practices. The parties select the neutral best qualified to hear their controversy.

## Cost

The administrative fees of the AAA and the compensation arrangements for the neutral are set forth in the particular dispute resolution agreed on. Fees are posted on the AAA's website (www.adr.org) and pamphlets containing the various procedures are available from any AAA regional office.

## Administrative Fees

The nonrefundable case set-up fee is $150 per party. An AAA administrative fee of $75 per every hour of conference time spent by the mediator is also charged. The $150 nonrefundable case set-up fees will be applied toward the AAA administrative fee. In addition, the parties are responsible for compensating the mediator at his or her published rate, for conference and study time (hourly or per diem).

All expenses are generally borne equally by the parties. The parties may adjust this arrangement by agreement.

Before the commencement of the mediation, the AAA shall estimate anticipated total expenses. Each party shall pay its portion of that amount as per the agreed upon arrangement. When the mediation has terminated, the AAA shall render an accounting and return any unexpended balance to the parties.

### Initiation Under A Submission

Parties to any existing dispute may commence an arbitration under these rules by filing at any office of the AAA two copies of a written submission to arbitrate under these rules, signed by the parties. It shall contain a statement of the nature of the dispute, the names and addresses of all parties, any claims and counterclaims, the amount involved, if any, the remedy sought, and the hearing locale requested, together with the appropriate filing fees as provided in the schedule included with these rules. Unless the parties state otherwise in the submission, all claims and counterclaims will be deemed to be denied by the other party.

# Commercial Mediation Rules

## Introduction

The American Arbitration Association (AAA), a not-for-profit, public service organization, offers a broad range of dispute resolution services to business executives, attorneys, individuals, trade associations, unions, management, consumers, families, communities, and all levels of government. Services are available through AAA headquarters in New York and through offices located in major cities throughout the United States. Hearings may be held at locations convenient for the parties and are not limited to cities with AAA offices. In addition, the AAA serves as a center for education and training, issues specialized publications, and conducts research on all forms of out-of-court dispute settlement.

## Mediation

The parties might wish to submit their dispute to mediation prior to arbitration. In mediation, the neutral mediator assists the parties in reaching a settlement but does not have the authority to make a binding decision or award. Mediation is administered by the AAA in accordance with its Commercial Mediation Rules. There is no additional administrative fee where parties to a pending arbitration attempt to mediate their dispute under the AAA's auspices.

If the parties want to adopt mediation as a part of their contractual dispute settlement procedure, they can insert the following mediation clause into their contract in conjunction with a standard arbitration provision:

*If a dispute arises out of or relates to this contract, or the breach thereof, and if the dispute cannot be settled through negotiation, the parties agree first to try in good faith to settle the dispute by mediation administered by the American Arbitration Association under its Commercial Mediation Rules before resorting to arbitration, litigation, or some other dispute resolution procedure.*

If the parties want to use a mediator to resolve an existing dispute, they can enter into the following submission:

*The parties hereby submit the following dispute to mediation administered by the American Arbitration Association under its Commercial Mediation Rules. (The clause may also provide for the qualifications of the mediator(s), method of payment, locale of meetings, and any other item of concern to the parties.)*

## COMMERCIAL MEDIATION RULES

### M-1. Agreement of Parties

Whenever, by stipulation or in their contract, the parties have provided for mediation or conciliation of existing or future disputes under the auspices of the American Arbitration Association (AAA) or under these rules, they shall be deemed to have made these rules, as amended and in effect as of the date of the submission of the dispute, a part of their agreement.

## M-2. Initiation of Mediation

Any party or parties to a dispute may initiate mediation by filing with the AAA a submission to mediation or a written request for mediation pursuant to these rules, together with the appropriate Filing Fee (page 13). Where there is no submission to mediation or contract providing for mediation, a party may request the AAA to invite another party to join in a submission to mediation. Upon receipt of such a request, the AAA will contact the other parties involved in the dispute and attempt to obtain a submission to mediation.

## M-3. Requests for Mediation

A request for mediation shall contain a brief statement of the nature of the dispute and the names, addresses, and telephone numbers of all parties to the dispute and those who will represent them, if any, in the mediation. The initiating party shall simultaneously file two copies of the request with the AAA and one copy with every other party to the dispute.

## M-4. Appointment of the Mediator

Upon receipt of a request for mediation, the AAA will appoint a qualified mediator to serve. Normally, a single mediator will be appointed unless the parties agree otherwise or the AAA determines otherwise. If the agreement of the parties names a mediator or specifies a method of appointing a mediator, that designation or method shall be followed.

## M-5. Qualifications of the Mediator

No person shall serve as a mediator in any dispute in which that person has any financial or personal interest in the result of the mediation, except by the written consent of all parties. Prior to accepting an appointment, the prospective mediator shall disclose any circumstance likely to create a presumption of bias or prevent a prompt meeting with the parties. Upon receipt of such information, the AAA shall either replace the mediator or immediately communicate the information to the parties for their comments. In the event that the parties disagree as to whether the mediator shall serve, the AAA will appoint another mediator.

The AAA is authorized to appoint another mediator if the appointed mediator is unable to serve promptly.

## M-6. Vacancies

If any mediator shall become unwilling or unable to serve, the AAA will appoint another mediator, unless the parties agree otherwise.

## M-7. Representation

Any party may be represented by persons of the party's choice. The names and addresses of such persons shall be communicated in writing to all parties and to the AAA.

## M-8. Date, Time, and Place of Mediation

The mediator shall fix the date and the time of each mediation session. The mediation shall be held at the appropriate regional office of the AAA, or at any other convenient location agreeable to the mediator and the parties, as the mediator shall determine.

## M-9. Identification of Matters in Dispute

At least ten days prior to the first scheduled mediation session, each party shall provide the mediator with a brief memorandum setting forth its position with regard to the issues that need to be resolved. At the discretion of the mediator, such memoranda may be mutually exchanged by the parties.

At the first session, the parties will be expected to produce all information reasonably required for the mediator to understand the issues presented.

The mediator may require any party to supplement such information.

## M-10. Authority of the Mediator

The mediator does not have the authority to impose a settlement on the parties but will attempt to help them reach a satisfactory resolution of their dispute. The mediator is authorized to conduct joint and separate meetings with the parties and to make oral and written recommendations for settlement. Whenever necessary, the mediator may also obtain expert advice concerning technical aspects of the dispute, provided that the parties agree and assume the expenses of obtaining such advice. Arrangements for obtaining such advice shall be made by the mediator or the parties, as the mediator shall determine.

The mediator is authorized to end the mediation whenever, in the judgment of the mediator, further efforts at mediation would not contribute to a resolution of the dispute between the parties.

## M-11. Privacy

Mediation sessions are private. The parties and their representatives may attend mediation sessions. Other persons may attend only with the permission of the parties and with the consent of the mediator.

## M-12. Confidentiality

Confidential information disclosed to a mediator by the parties or by witnesses in the course of the mediation shall not be divulged by the mediator. All records, reports, or other documents received by a mediator while serving in that capacity shall be confidential. The mediator shall not be compelled to divulge such records or to testify in regard to the mediation in any adversary proceeding or judicial forum.

The parties shall maintain the confidentiality of the mediation and shall not rely on, or introduce as evidence in any arbitral, judicial, or other proceeding:

a. views expressed or suggestions made by another party with respect to a possible settlement of the dispute;

b.  admissions made by another party in the course of the mediation proceedings;
c.  proposals made or views expressed by the mediator; or
d.  the fact that another party had or had not indicated willingness to accept a proposal for settlement made by the mediator.

## M-13. No Stenographic Record

There shall be no stenographic record of the mediation process.

## M-14. Termination of Mediation

The mediation shall be terminated:

a.  by the execution of a settlement agreement by the parties;
b.  by a written declaration of the mediator to the effect that further efforts at mediation are no longer worthwhile; or
c.  by a written declaration of a party or parties to the effect that the mediation proceedings are terminated.

## M-15. Exclusion of Liability

Neither the AAA nor any mediator is a necessary party in judicial proceedings relating to the mediation.

Neither the AAA nor any mediator shall be liable to any party for any act or omission in connection with any mediation conducted under these rules.

## M-16. Interpretation and Application of Rules

The mediator shall interpret and apply these rules insofar as they relate to the mediator's duties and responsibilities. All other rules shall be interpreted and applied by the AAA.

## M-17. Expenses

The expenses of witnesses for either side shall be paid by the party producing such witnesses. All other expenses of the mediation, including required traveling and other expenses of the mediator and representatives of the AAA, and the expenses of any witness and the cost of any proofs or expert advice produced at the direct request of the mediator, shall be borne equally by the parties unless they agree otherwise.

## ADMINISTRATIVE FEES

The nonrefundable case set-up fee is $150 per party. An AAA administrative fee of $75 per every hour of conference time spent by the mediator is also charged. The $150 nonrefundable case set-up fees will be applied toward the AAA administrative fee. In addition, the parties are responsible for compensating the mediator at his or her published rate, for conference and study time (hourly or per diem).

All expenses are generally borne equally by the parties. The parties may adjust this arrangement by agreement.

Before the commencement of the mediation, the AAA shall estimate anticipated total expenses. Each party shall pay its portion of that amount as per the agreed upon arrangement. When the mediation has terminated, the AAA shall render an accounting and return any unexpended balance to the parties.

Rules, forms, procedures and guides, as well as information about applying for a fee reduction or deferral, are subject to periodic change and updating. To ensure that you have the most current information, see our Web site at www.adr.org

# APPENDIX E

## THE CPR MEDIATION PROCEDURE (Revised 1998)

## 1.     AGREEMENT TO MEDIATE

The CPR Mediation Procedure (the "Procedure") may be adopted by agreement of the parties, with or without modification, before or after a dispute has arisen. The following provisions are suggested:

### A.        Pre-dispute Clause

The parties shall attempt in good faith to resolve any dispute arising out of or relating to this Agreement promptly by confidential mediation under the [then current] CPR Mediation Procedure [in effect on the date of this Agreement], before resorting to arbitration or litigation.

### B.        Existing Dispute Submission Agreement

We hereby agree to submit to confidential mediation under the CPR Mediation Procedure the following controversy:

(Describe briefly)

## 2.    SELECTING THE MEDIATOR

Unless the parties agree otherwise, the mediator shall be selected from the CPR Panels of Neutrals. If the parties cannot agree promptly on a mediator, they will notify CPR of their need for assistance in selecting a mediator, informing CPR of any preferences as to matters such as candidates' mediation style, subject matter expertise and geographic location. CPR will submit to the parties the names of not less than three candidates, with their resumes and hourly rates. If the parties are unable to agree on a candidate from the list within seven days following receipt of the list, each party will, within 15 days following receipt of the list, send to CPR the list of candidates ranked in descending order of preference. The candidate with the lowest combined score will be appointed as the mediator by CPR. CPR will break any tie.

Before proposing any mediator candidate, CPR will request the candidate to disclose any circumstances known to him or her that would cause reasonable doubt regarding the candidate's impartiality. If a clear conflict is disclosed, the individual will not be proposed. Other circumstances a candidate discloses to CPR will be disclosed to the parties. A party may challenge a mediator candidate if it knows of any circumstances giving rise to reasonable doubt regarding the candidate's impartiality.

The mediator's rate of compensation will be determined before appointment. Such compensation, and any other costs of the process, will be shared equally by the parties unless they otherwise agree. If a party withdraws from a multiparty mediation but the procedure continues, the withdrawing party will not be responsible for any costs incurred after it has notified the mediator and the other parties of its withdrawal.

Before appointment, the mediator will assure the parties of his or her availability to conduct the proceeding expeditiously. It is strongly advised that the parties and the mediator enter into a retention agreement.

# 3. GROUND RULES OF PROCEEDING

The following ground rules will apply, subject to any changes on which the parties and the mediator agree.

(a) The process is non-binding.

(b) Each party may withdraw at any time after attending the first session, and before execution of a written settlement agreement, by written notice to the mediator and the other party or parties.

(c) The mediator shall be neutral and impartial.

(d) The mediator shall control the procedural aspects of the mediation. The parties will cooperate fully with the mediator.

   i. The mediator is free to meet and communicate separately with each party.

   ii. The mediator will decide when to hold joint meetings with the parties and when to hold separate meetings. The mediator will fix the time and place of each session and its agenda in consultation with the parties. There will be no stenographic record of any meeting. Formal rules of evidence or procedure will not apply.

(e) Each party will be represented at each mediation conference by a business executive authorized to negotiate a resolution of the dispute, unless excused by the mediator as to a particular conference. Each party may be represented by more than one person, e.g., a business executive and an attorney. The mediator may limit the number of persons representing each party.

(f)    Each party will be represented by counsel to advise it in the mediation, whether or not such counsel is present at mediation conferences.

(g)    The process will be conducted expeditiously. Each representative will make every effort to be available for meetings.

(h)    The mediator will not transmit information received in confidence from any party to any other party or any third party unless authorized to do so by the party transmitting the information, or unless ordered to do so by a court of competent jurisdiction.

(i)    Unless the parties agree otherwise, they will refrain from pursuing litigation or any administrative or judicial remedies during the mediation process or for a set period of time, insofar as they can do so without prejudicing their legal rights.

(j)    Unless all parties and the mediator otherwise agree in writing, the mediator and any persons assisting the mediator will be disqualified as a witness, consultant or expert in any pending or future investigation, action or proceeding relating to the subject matter of the mediation (including any investigation, action or proceeding which involves persons not party to this mediation).

(k)    If the dispute goes into arbitration, the mediator shall not serve as an arbitrator, unless the parties and the mediator otherwise agree in writing.

(l)    The mediator may obtain assistance and independent expert advice, with the prior agreement of and at the expense of the parties. Any person proposed as an independent expert also will be required to disclose any circumstances known to him or her that would cause reasonable doubt regarding the candidate's impartiality.

(m)     Neither CPR nor the mediator shall be liable for any act or omission in connection with the mediation, except for its/his/her own willful misconduct.

(n)     The mediator may withdraw at any time by written notice to the parties (i) for serious personal reasons, (ii) if the mediator believes that a party is not acting in good faith, or (iii) if the mediator concludes that further mediation efforts would not be useful. If the mediator withdraws pursuant to (i) or (ii), he or she need not state the reason for withdrawal.

# 4.     EXCHANGE OF INFORMATION

If any party has a substantial need for documents or other material in the possession of another party, or for other discovery that may facilitate a settlement, the parties shall attempt to agree thereon. Should they fail to agree, either party may request a joint consultation with the mediator who shall assist the parties in reaching agreement.

The parties shall exchange with each other, with a copy to the mediator, the names and job titles of all individuals who will attend the joint mediation session.

At the conclusion of the mediation process, upon the request of a party which provided documents or other material to one or more other parties, the recipients shall return the same to the originating party without retaining copies.

# 5.     PRESENTATION TO THE MEDIATOR

Before dealing with the substance of the dispute, the parties and the mediator will discuss preliminary matters, such as possible modification of the procedure, place and time of meetings, and each party's need for documents or other information in the possession of the other.

At least 10 business days before the first substantive mediation conference, unless otherwise agreed, each party will submit to the mediator a written statement summarizing the background and present status of the dispute, including any settlement efforts that have occurred, and such other material and information as the mediator requests or the party deems helpful to familiarize the mediator with the dispute. It is desirable for the submission to include an analysis of the party's real interests and needs and of its litigation risks. The parties may agree to submit jointly certain records and other materials. The mediator may request any party to provide clarification and additional information.

The parties are encouraged to discuss the exchange of all or certain materials they submit to the mediator to further each party's understanding of the other party's viewpoints. The mediator may request the parties to submit a joint statement of facts. Except as the parties otherwise agree, the mediator shall keep confidential any written materials or information that are submitted to him or her. The parties and their representatives are not entitled to receive or review any materials or information submitted to the mediator by another party or representative without the concurrence of the latter. At the conclusion of the mediation process, upon request of a party, the mediator will return to that party all written materials and information which that party had provided to the mediator without retaining copies thereof or certify as to the destruction of such materials.

At the first substantive mediation conference each party will make an opening statement.

## 6.  NEGOTIATIONS

The mediator may facilitate settlement in any manner the mediator believes is appropriate. The mediator will help the parties focus on their underlying interests and concerns, explore resolution alternatives and develop settlement options. The mediator will decide when to hold joint meetings, and when to confer separately with each party.

The parties are expected to initiate and convey to the mediator proposals for settlement. Each party shall provide a rationale for any settlement terms proposed.

Finally, if the parties fail to develop mutually acceptable settlement terms, before terminating the procedure, and only with the consent of the parties, (a) the mediator may submit to the parties a final settlement proposal; and (b) if the mediator believes he/she is qualified to do so, the mediator may give the parties an evaluation (which if all parties choose, and the mediator agrees, may be in writing) of the likely outcome of the case if it were tried to final judgment. Thereupon, the mediator may suggest further discussions to explore whether the mediator's evaluation or proposal may lead to a resolution.

Efforts to reach a settlement will continue until (a) a written settlement is reached, or (b) the mediator concludes and informs the parties that further efforts would not be useful, or (c) one of the parties or the mediator withdraws from the process. However, if there are more than two parties, the remaining parties may elect to continue following the withdrawal of a party.

## 7.    SETTLEMENT

If a settlement is reached, a preliminary memorandum of understanding or term sheet normally will be prepared and signed or initialed before the parties separate. Thereafter, unless the mediator undertakes to do so, representatives of the parties will promptly draft a written settlement document incorporating all settlement terms. This draft will be circulated, amended as necessary, and formally executed. If litigation is pending, the settlement may provide that the parties will request dismissal of the case. The parties also may request the court to enter the settlement agreement as a consent judgment.

## 8.    FAILURE TO AGREE

If a resolution is not reached, the mediator will discuss with the parties the possibility of their agreeing on advisory or binding arbitration, "last offer" arbitration or another form of ADR. If the parties agree in principle, the mediator may offer to assist them in structuring a procedure designed to result in a prompt, economical process. The mediator will not serve as arbitrator, unless all parties agree.

## 9.    CONFIDENTIALITY

The entire mediation process is confidential. Unless agreed among all the parties or required to do so by law, the parties and the mediator shall not disclose to any person who is not associated with participants in the process, including any judicial officer, any information regarding the process (including pre-process exchanges and agreements), contents (including written and oral information), settlement terms or outcome of the proceeding. If litigation is pending, the participants may, however, advise the court of the schedule and overall status of the mediation for purposes of litigation management. Any written settlement agreement resulting from the mediation may be disclosed for purposes of enforcement.

Under this procedure, the entire process is a compromise negotiation subject to Federal Rule of Evidence 408 and all state counterparts, together with any applicable statute protecting the confidentiality of mediation. All offers, promises, conduct and statements, whether oral or written, made in the course of the proceeding by any of the parties, their agents, employees, experts and attorneys, and by the mediator are confidential. Such offers, promises, conduct and statements are privileged under any applicable mediation privilege and are inadmissible and not discoverable for any purpose, including impeachment, in litigation between the parties. However, evidence that is otherwise admissible or discoverable shall not be rendered inadmissible or non-discoverable solely as a result of its presentation or use during the mediation.

The exchange of any tangible material shall be without prejudice to any claim that such material is privileged or protected as work-product within the meaning of Federal Rule of Civil Procedure 26 and all state and local counterparts.

The mediator and any documents and information in the mediator's possession will not be subpoenaed in any such investigation, action or proceeding, and all parties will oppose any effort to have the mediator or documents subpoenaed. The mediator will promptly advise the parties of any attempt to compel him/her to divulge information received in mediation.

# APPENDIX F

## MODEL STANDARDS OF CONDUCT FOR MEDIATORS

## (ABA, AAA AND SPIDR)[1]

### AMERICAN ARBITRATION ASSOCIATION

### AMERICAN BAR ASSOCIATION

### SOCIETY OF PROFESSIONALS IN DISPUTE RESOLUTION

Reprinted with permission of AAA, ABA and SPIDR

The Model Standards of Conduct for Mediators were prepared from 1992 through 1994 by a joint committee composed of two delegates from the American Arbitration Association, John D. Feerick, Chair, and David Botwinik, two from the American Bar Association, James Alfini and Nancy Rogers, and two from the Society of Professionals in Dispute Resolution, Susan Dearborn and Lemoine Pierce.

The Model Standards have been approved by the American Arbitration Association, the Litigation Section and the Dispute Resolution Section of the American Bar Association, and the Society of Professionals in Dispute Resolution.

Reporters: Bryant Garth and Kimberlee K. Kovach
Staff Project Director: Frederick E. Woods

The views set out in this publication have not been considered by the American Bar Association House of Delegates and do not constitute the policy of the American Bar Association.

---

[1] SPIDR has merged with other organizations and is now know as ACR (Association for Conflict Resolution). ACR is a professional organization dedicated to enhancing the practice and public understanding of conflict resolution.

> **MODEL STANDARDS OF**
> **CONDUCT FOR MEDIATORS**

## Introductory Note

The initiative for these standards came from three professional groups: the American Arbitration Association, the American Bar Association, and the Society of Professionals in Dispute Resolution.

The purpose of this initiative was to develop a set of standards to serve as a general framework for the practice of mediation. The effort is a step in the development of the field and a tool to assist practitioners in it—a beginning, not an end. The model standards are intended to apply to all types of mediation. It is recognized, however, that in some cases the application of these standards may be affected by laws or contractual agreements.

## Preface

The model standards of conduct for mediators are intended to perform three major functions: to serve as a guide for the conduct of mediators; to inform the mediating parties; and to promote public confidence in mediation as a process for resolving disputes. The standards draw on existing codes of conduct for mediators and take into account issues and problems that have surfaced in mediation practice. They are offered in the hope that they will serve an educational function and provide assistance to individuals, organizations, and institutions involved in mediation.

Mediation is a process in which an impartial third party—a mediator—facilitates the resolution of a dispute by promoting voluntary agreement (or "self-determination") by the parties to the dispute. A mediator facilitates communications, promotes understanding, focuses the parties on their interests, and seeks creative problem-solving to enable the parties to reach their own agreement. These standards give meaning to this definition of mediation.

## I.  Self-Determination:  A Mediator Shall Recognize That Mediation Is Based on the Principle of Self-Determination by the Parties.

Self-determination is the fundamental principle of mediation. It requires that the mediation process rely upon the ability of the parties to reach a voluntary, uncoerced agreement. Any party may withdraw from mediation at any time.

### COMMENTS:

• The mediator may provide information about the process, raise issues, and help parties explore options. The primary role of the mediator is to facilitate a voluntary resolution of a dispute. Parties shall be given the opportunity to consider all proposed options.

• A mediator cannot personally ensure that each party has made a fully informed choice to reach a particular agreement, but it is a good practice for the mediator to make the parties aware of the importance of consulting other professionals, where appropriate, to help them make informed decisions.

## II.  Impartiality: A Mediator Shall Conduct the Mediation in an Impartial Manner.

The concept of mediator impartiality is central to the mediation process. A mediator shall mediate only those matters in which she or he can remain impartial and evenhanded. If at any time the mediator is unable to conduct the process in an impartial manner, the mediator is obligated to withdraw.

**COMMENTS:**

• A mediator shall avoid conduct that gives the appearance of partiality toward one of the parties. The quality of the mediation process is enhanced when the parties have confidence in the impartiality of the mediator.

• When mediators are appointed by a court or institution, the appointing agency shall make reasonable efforts to ensure that mediators serve impartially.

• A mediator should guard against partiality or prejudice based on the parties' personal characteristics, background or performance at the mediation.

## III. Conflicts of Interest: A Mediator Shall Disclose All Actual and Potential Conflicts of Interest Reasonably Known to the Mediator. After Disclosure, the Mediator Shall Decline to Mediate Unless All Parties Choose to Retain the Mediator. The Need to Protect Against Conflicts of Interest Also Governs Conduct That Occurs During and After the Mediation.

A conflict of interest is a dealing or relationship that might create an impression of possible bias. The basic approach to questions of conflict of interest is consistent with the concept of self-determination. The mediator has a responsibility to disclose all actual and potential conflicts that are reasonably known to the mediator and could reasonably be seen as raising a question about impartiality. If all parties agree to mediate after being informed of conflicts, the mediator may proceed with the mediation. If, however, the conflict of interest casts serious doubt on the integrity of the process, the mediator shall decline to proceed.

A mediator must avoid the appearance of conflict of interest both during and after the mediation. Without the consent of all parties, a mediator shall not subsequently establish a professional relationship with one of the parties in a related matter, or in an unrelated matter under circumstances which would raise legitimate questions about the integrity of the mediation process.

### COMMENTS:

• A mediator shall avoid conflicts of interest in recommending the services of other professionals. A mediator may make reference to professional referral services or associations which maintain rosters of qualified professionals.

• Potential conflicts of interest may arise between administrators of mediation programs and mediators and there may be strong pressures on the mediator to settle a particular case or cases. The mediator's commitment must be to the parties and the process. Pressure from outside of the mediation process should never influence the mediator to coerce parties to settle.

## IV.    Competence: A Mediator Shall Mediate Only When the Mediator Has the Necessary Qualifications to Satisfy the Reasonable Expectations of the Parties.

Any person may be selected as a mediator, provided that the parties are satisfied with the mediator's qualifications. Training and experience in mediation, however, are often necessary for effective mediation. A person who offers herself or himself as available to serve as a mediator gives parties and the public the expectation that she or he has the competency to mediate effectively. In court-connected or other forms of mandated mediation, it is essential that mediators assigned to the parties have the requisite training and experience.

**COMMENTS:**

• Mediators should have information available for the parties regarding their relevant training, education and experience.

• The requirements for appearing on a list of mediators must be made public and available to interested persons.

• When mediators are appointed by a court or institution, the appointing agency shall make reasonable efforts to ensure that each mediator is qualified for the particular mediation.

## V. Confidentiality: A Mediator Shall Maintain the Reasonable Expectations of the Parties with Regard to Confidentiality.

The reasonable expectations of the parties with regard to confidentiality shall be met by the mediator. The parties' expectations of confidentiality depend on the circumstances of the mediation and any agreements they may make. The mediator shall not disclose any matter that a party expects to be confidential unless given permission by all parties or unless required by law or other public policy.

**COMMENTS:**

• The parties may make their own rules with respect to confidentiality, or the accepted practice of an individual mediator or institution may dictate a particular set of expectations. Since the parties' expectations regarding confidentiality are important, the mediator should discuss these expectations with the parties.

• If the mediator holds private sessions with a party, the nature of these sessions with regard to confidentiality should be discussed prior to undertaking such sessions.

- In order to protect the integrity of the mediation, a mediator should avoid communicating information about how the parties acted in the mediation process, the merits of the case, or settlement offers. The mediator may report, if required, whether parties appeared at a scheduled mediation.

- Where the parties have agreed that all or a portion of the information disclosed during a mediation is confidential, the parties' agreement should be respected by the mediator.

- Confidentiality should not be construed to limit or prohibit the effective monitoring, research, or evaluation of mediation programs by responsible persons. Under appropriate circumstances, researchers may be permitted to obtain access to statistical data and, with the permission of the parties, to individual case files, observations of live mediations, and interviews with participants.

## VI. Quality of the Process: A Mediator Shall Conduct the Mediation Fairly, Diligently, and in a Manner Consistent with the Principle of Self-Determination by the Parties.

A mediator shall work to ensure a quality process and to encourage mutual respect among the parties. A quality process requires a commitment by the mediator to diligence and procedural fairness. There should be adequate opportunity for each party in the mediation to participate in the discussions. The parties decide when and under what conditions they will reach an agreement or terminate a mediation.

**COMMENTS:**

- A mediator may agree to mediate only when he or she is prepared to commit the attention essential to an effective mediation.

• Mediators should only accept cases when they can satisfy the reasonable expectations of the parties concerning the timing of the process. A mediator should not allow a mediation to be unduly delayed by the parties or their representatives.

• The presence or absence of persons at a mediation depends on the agreement of the parties and mediator. The parties and mediator may agree that others may be excluded from particular sessions or from the entire mediation process.

• The primary purpose of a mediator is to facilitate the parties' voluntary agreement. This role differs substantially from other professional-client relationships. Mixing the role of a mediator and the role of a professional advising a client is problematic, and mediators must strive to distinguish between the roles. A mediator should, therefore, refrain from providing professional advice. Where appropriate, a mediator should recommend that parties seek outside professional advice, or consider resolving their dispute through arbitration, counseling, neutral evaluation, or other processes. A mediator who undertakes, at the request of the parties, an additional dispute resolution role in the same matter assumes increased responsibilities and obligations that may be governed by the standards of other professions.

• A mediator shall withdraw from a mediation when incapable of serving or when unable to remain impartial.

• A mediator shall withdraw from a mediation or postpone a session if the mediation is being used to further illegal conduct, or if a party is unable to participate due to drug, alcohol, or other physical or mental incapacity.

• Mediators should not permit their behavior in the mediation process to be guided by a desire for a high settlement rate.

## VII. Advertising and Solicitation: A Mediator Shall Be Truthful in Advertising and Solicitation for Mediation.

Advertising or any other communication with the public concerning services offered or regarding the education, training, and expertise of the mediator shall be truthful. Mediators shall refrain from promises and guarantees of results.

### COMMENTS:

• It is imperative that communication with the public educate and instill confidence in the process.

• In an advertisement or other communication to the public, a mediator may make reference to meeting state, national, or private organization qualifications only if the entity referred to has a procedure for qualifying mediators and the mediator has been duly granted the requisite status.

## VIII. Fees: A Mediator Shall Fully Disclose and Explain the Basis of Compensation, Fees, and Charges to the Parties.

The parties should be provided sufficient information about fees at the outset of a mediation to determine if they wish to retain the services of a mediator. If a mediator charges fees, the fees shall be reasonable, considering, among other things, the mediation service, the type and complexity of the matter, the expertise of the mediator, the time required, and the rates customary in the community. The better practice in reaching an understanding about fees is to set down the arrangements in a written agreement.

**COMMENTS:**

• A mediator who withdraws from a mediation should return any unearned fee to the parties.

• A mediator should not enter into a fee agreement which is contingent upon the result of the mediation or amount of the settlement.

• Co-mediators who share a fee should hold to standards of reasonableness in determining the allocation of fees.

• A mediator should not accept a fee for referral of a matter to another mediator or to any other person.

## IX.   Obligations to the Mediation Process: Mediators Have a Duty to Improve the Practice of Mediation.

**COMMENT:**

• Mediators are regarded as knowledgeable in the process of mediation. They have an obligation to use their knowledge to help educate the public about mediation; to make mediation accessible to those who would like to use it; to correct abuses; and to improve their professional skills and abilities.

# APPENDIX G
## BICKERMAN DISPUTE RESOLUTION GROUP
## MEDIATION AGREEMENT

Reprinted with permission of Bickerman Dispute Resolution Group

MEDIATION AGREEMENT

BETWEEN

PARTY
AND
PARTY

The parties whose signatures are affixed below hereby agree to the terms and conditions of this Mediation Agreement.

## I.  Purpose and Responsibilities

The purpose of the mediation will be to attempt to arrive cooperatively and informally at a mutually acceptable resolution of the dispute.

## II.  Mediation Process

### A.  Overview

John Bickerman will serve as mediator and may be assisted by others as reasonably necessary at his discretion to serve the parties and accomplish the objectives of this Agreement. The mediator may review written information submitted by the parties and counsel. He may also communicate *ex parte* with mediation participants.

The mediator will meet with counsel on **[DATE]** at the offices of **[LOCATION]**, from **[TIME]**. After this initial meeting, the mediator may also conduct private, confidential meetings with the parties.

The initial joint mediation session will take place at the offices of **[LOCATION]**, beginning at **[TIME AND DATE]** and concluding no later than **[TIME AND DATE]**.

The joint mediation session shall be attended by party representatives with full settlement authority. During the joint mediation session, representatives of the parties may be expected to briefly present their positions on the issues in dispute and respond to the other **[party's; parties']** positions. These summary presentations may be made by counsel or representatives of the parties. No rules of evidence will apply.

After the summary presentations, the mediator may meet separately and together, as necessary, with the parties, counsel and other participants to assist them in resolving the dispute. If the dispute is not settled after the joint mediation session the mediator may continue individual discussions by telephone or in person.

## B.     Procedure

### 1.     Confidential Statement of Claims and Positions

As agreed, no later than **[DATE],** the parties shall submit to the mediator a confidential statement of approximately **[number]** pages setting forth key facts and their claims, positions and contentions in this dispute. In addition, each statement should project for what the opposing party would be willing to settle. These confidential statements shall not be shared with any other party and shall be used solely to assist the mediator in his work.

### 2.     Party Representatives

Unless the parties agree otherwise, representatives of each party having full settlement authority shall participate in all phases of the mediation process directly, by telephone or through periodic reporting by counsel. At the **[DATE]** meeting, each party shall provide the mediator and the other parties the names of the representative(s) participating at the joint mediation session on its behalf. The mediator may consult with the parties concerning these designated representatives, their settlement authority, and level of participation in various phases of the process.

## III. Destruction of Documents

Forty-five (45) days after the conclusion of the mediation, the mediator will destroy all of his copies of all materials sent or provided to the mediator by the parties, including confidential statements, confidential communications, pleadings and other documents, including but not limited to audio/visual tapes and electronic mail (e-mail) transmissions, to protect the confidential nature of the mediation. The mediator will retain a copy of the settlement agreement, if a settlement is reached.

## IV. No Legal Advice Rendered By The Mediator

The parties to the mediation represent that they have obtained legal counsel to advise them during the mediation. The mediator will not provide legal advice.

## V. Conflicts of Interest

### A. Disclosure of Prior Relationships

The mediator has made a reasonable effort to learn and has disclosed to the parties: (a) all business or professional relationships the mediator and/or the mediator's firm has had with the parties or their law firms within the past three years; (b) any financial interest the mediator has in any party; (c) any significant social, business or professional relationship the mediator has had with an officer or employee of a party or with an individual representing a party in the mediation; and (d) any other circumstances that may create doubt regarding the mediator's impartiality in the mediation.

Each party and its law firm has made a reasonable effort to learn and has disclosed to every other party and the mediator any relationships of a nature described in the preceding paragraph not previously identified and disclosed by the mediator.

The parties and the mediator are satisfied that any relationships disclosed pursuant to the preceding paragraphs will not affect the mediator's independence or impartiality. Notwithstanding any such relationships, the parties have chosen the mediator to serve in the mediation, waiving any claim based on such relationships, and the mediator agrees to so serve.

## B.   Future Relationships

Neither the mediator nor the mediator's firm shall undertake any work for or against a party regarding the subject matter of the mediation. The mediator's firm may mediate other matters involving one or more of the parties during the pendency of the mediation.

## VI.   Confidentiality

This entire mediation process is a compromise negotiation. All offers, promises, conduct, and statements, whether oral or written, made in the course of the mediation by the parties, their agents, employees, experts and attorneys, and the mediator are confidential. Such offers, promises, conduct, and statements will not be disclosed to third parties, except persons associated with the parties in the mediation process and persons or entities to whom a party has a legal or contractual obligation to report, and are privileged and inadmissible for any purpose, including impeachment, under Rule 408 of the Federal Rules of Evidence and any applicable federal or state statute, rule or common law provisions. All information, reports, data and/or documents prepared by or on behalf of the parties, and/or presented to the mediator, are deemed confidential and shall not be disclosed. However, evidence previously disclosed or known to a party, or that is otherwise admissible or discoverable, shall not be rendered confidential, inadmissible, or not discoverable solely as a result of its use in the mediation. Furthermore, **[party's; parties']** experts who participate in this mediation shall not be disqualified from assisting a party in subsequent litigation concerning the subject of the dispute of this mediation.

## VII.   Settlement Agreement

Any resolution of the dispute shall be reduced to writing and executed by the parties. Parties are advised to have the settlement agreement independently reviewed by their own counsel prior to executing the agreement.

## VIII. Disqualification of Mediator

Neither John Bickerman, nor any person who assists him, is a necessary party in any arbitral or judicial proceeding relating to the mediation or to the subject matter of this dispute. Neither John Bickerman, nor any person who assists him, may be called as a witness or an expert in any pending or subsequent litigation or arbitration involving the parties and relating to this dispute. Moreover, John Bickerman and any person who assists him will be disqualified as witnesses or as experts in any pending or subsequent litigation or arbitration relating to this dispute.

## IX.   Mediation Costs

### A.     Explanation of Mediation Costs

Each party shall be responsible for payment of its share of the mediator's fees and expenses. These will include the mediator's fees at his standard mediation rate. Professional fees for joint sessions are charged at the rate of $5,000 per day. Preparation, pre- and post- mediation follow-up are billed at the rate of $500 per hour.

Mediation fees represent charges for time spent with the parties, time required to study documents, research issues, correspond, make telephone calls, prepare draft and final agreements, and do such other things as may be reasonably necessary to facilitate the parties' reaching full agreement. Mediation fees may also include the time required to travel to individual meetings or joint mediation sessions.

### B.    Cancellation/Rescheduling Charge

A cancellation fee of up to eight hours may be charged for sessions that are cancelled by the parties within thirty (30) business days of the initial joint session, unless the time can be rescheduled. A rescheduling charge of up to four hours may be charged for sessions that are rescheduled by the parties within thirty (30) business days of the initial joint session, unless the time can be rescheduled. Actual expenses are billed at cost.

### C.    Case Management Fee

The Case Management Fee covers certain costs associated with the mediation, such as case scheduling, establishment of files, document handling, copying, faxing and overnight mailing, use of Bickerman Dispute Resolution, PLLC conference facilities and regular telephone usage (conference calls with multiple parties are billed at actual cost).

The Case Management Fee is 6% of total professional fees.

### D.    Rescheduling Fees

Fees for mediation sessions cancelled more than 30 days in advance of a session are fully refundable. The parties are charged for sessions cancelled less than 30 days before a session, unless the time can be rescheduled for another matter.

No rescheduling fee will be charged for cases that are rescheduled more than 30 days in advance of a session. A rescheduling fee of 50% will be charged for sessions rescheduled less than 30 days before a session.

If a mediation session is completed in less time than was budgeted, the actual time reserved but not used will be billed unless the time can be used for another matter.

### E.    Share of Mediation Costs

The responsibility for payment of the mediator's fees and expenses shall be divided equally between the parties to the mediation.

### F.    Retainer

Each party shall pay a retainer of $_____ **by __[DATE]__**. The retainers paid by each party shall be kept in a separate account and applied to fees after the parties have been provided with an invoice.

### G.    Payment of Invoices

All fees are due and payable upon receipt of the retainer invoice and must be paid for in advance of the initial joint mediation session. The parties agree to pay the amounts indicated in invoices they receive from the mediator (in excess of their retainers) within thirty days of the receipt of each invoice. If payment is not made within thirty days, the mediator reserves the right to charge interest at the rate of 1.5% per month.

## X.    Consent to Mediation

By their signatures below, the parties to the action hereby consent to mediation and agree to be bound by the terms and conditions of this Agreement.

By:_____    By:_____
Of:_____    Of:_____

Dated:_____    Dated:_____

# APPENDIX H

## JAMS MEDIATION AGREEMENT

**THE RESOLUTION EXPERTS**

### *SAMPLE* JAMS MEDIATION AGREEMENT
### Case Name: _____

## 1.     Mediation

***The Mediator's Role:***  The parties agree to submit the above-captioned matter for a non-binding mediation.  The parties understand that the role of the mediator is not to render a decision but to assist the parties in reaching a mutually acceptable resolution.

***Disclosure:***  The mediator, each party, and counsel confirm that they have disclosed any past or present relationship or other information that a reasonable person would believe would influence the mediator's impartiality.  The mediator practices in association with JAMS.  From time to time, JAMS may enter into arrangements with corporations (including insurance companies), government entities, and other organizations to make available dispute resolution professionals in a particular locale, for a specific type of matter or training, or for a particular period of time.  In addition, other professionals in JAMS may have served as neutrals in matters involving the parties hereto.  The mediator is not aware of any aspect of these relationships that would create a conflict or interfere with his/her acting as a mediator in this matter.

***Participants and Procedure:*** The mediation session will be attended by representatives of the parties with full settlement authority and may be attended by counsel. The parties will follow the recommendation of the mediator regarding the agenda most likely to resolve the dispute.

During the session, the mediator may have joint and separate meetings with the parties and their counsel. Private meetings will be confidential. If a party informs the mediator that information is conveyed by the party to the mediator in confidence, the mediator will not disclose the information.

At the discretion of the mediator or upon the request of the parties, the mediator will provide an evaluation of the parties' cases and of the likely resolution if the dispute is not settled. The parties agree that the mediator is not acting as an attorney or providing legal advice on behalf of any party.

The parties and/or their representatives will make themselves available for further discussions or meetings after the mediation session if such discussions are necessary or seem likely to be useful.

The parties agree to participate in good faith in the entire mediation process. If a party wishes to terminate its participation for any reason, it may do so by giving notice to JAMS and the other parties.

## 2. Confidentiality

This entire process is a compromise negotiation. All offers, promises, conduct and statements, whether oral or written, made in the course of the mediation by any of the parties, their agents, employees, experts and attorneys, and by the mediator and JAMS employees, who are the parties' joint agents and mediators for purposes of these compromise negotiations, are confidential. Such offers, promises, conduct, and statements (a) will not be disclosed to third parties (except persons associated with the participants in the process), and (b) are privileged and inadmissible for any purpose, including impeachment, under Rule 408 of the Federal Rules of Evidence and any applicable federal or state statute, rule or common law provisions. However, evidence previously disclosed or known to a party, or that is otherwise admissible or discoverable shall not be rendered confidential, inadmissible or not discoverable solely as a result of its use in the mediation.

## 3. Disqualification of Mediator and Exclusion of Liability

The parties agree not to call the mediator or any JAMS employee as a witness or as an expert in any pending or subsequent litigation or arbitration involving the parties and relating in any way to the dispute that is the subject of the mediation. The parties and JAMS agree that the mediator and any JAMS employee will be disqualified as a witness or as an expert in any pending or subsequent proceeding relating to the dispute that is the subject of the mediation. The parties agree to defend the mediator and JAMS from any subpoenas from outside parties arising out of this Agreement or mediation. The parties agree that neither the mediator nor JAMS is a necessary party in any arbitral or judicial proceeding relating to the mediation or to the subject matter of the mediation. Neither JAMS nor its employees or agents, including the mediator, shall be liable to any party for any act or omission in connection with any mediation conducted under this Agreement.

## 4.     Fees

The parties and their attorneys agree to pay JAMS as set forth in Appendix A, which is incorporated in this Agreement.

_____          _____

_____          _____

## JAMS Mediation Agreement

### APPENDIX A - Fee Agreement and Cancellation Policy for Ref. No._____

#### 1.    Professional Fees

Professional services for this mediation, including, but not limited to, reading and other preparation time, the mediation session, extra session time, and any additional services or work, will be billed at the mediator's normal hourly rate. Fees for unused scheduled time will not be refunded. The professional fee for ___(name of JAMS Neutral)___ is $____ per hour.

#### 2.    Additional Fees

A.    *Case Management Fees:* Each party will be charged a non-refundable Case Management Fee. The Case Management Fee includes case coordination, use of conference facilities, document handling (agreements, position statements, supporting materials, exhibits and briefs), copying, faxing, postage and administrative support. (Check with your local JAMS office for the Case Management Fee amount.)

B.    *Expenses:* Food and beverage costs incurred by the parties at the mediation will be invoiced to the parties at cost.

C.    *Travel:* If travel is required and is not included in a package rate, travel time is billed at the mediator's hourly rate. Travel expenses are billed at cost.

D.    *Reading/Research Fees:* Parties may be billed for expected reading and research time. Unused portions of these fees are refundable.

#### 3.    Cancellation and Rescheduling Policy

Fees for mediation sessions are non-refundable if a session is canceled or rescheduled less than 15 days before the original session date, unless the mediator's time can be rescheduled for other client work. Cancellation and rescheduling fees will be paid by the canceling party.

## 4.    Payment

    A.    Mediation fees and expenses will be divided equally or as agreed to by the parties.

    B.    Each party agrees to pay its share of the estimated fees prior to the mediation. The mediation will not be held unless such fees are paid. Unless it otherwise agrees, JAMS is not bound by agreements between or among the parties with respect to its fees.

    C.    Parties and counsel are separately liable for the payment of mediation fees and expenses.

BY: _____     BY: _____

FOR: _____     FOR: _____

DATED: _____     DATED: _____

# APPENDIX I

## ADR CLAUSES FOR BUSINESS AGREEMENTS (CPR)

This section offers detailed multistep clauses reflecting a variety of drafting options for more detailed agreements. If no binding resolution clause is included, litigation, by default, would remain the means of dispute resolution.

## PREAMBLE

Any dispute arising out of or relating to this Agreement shall be resolved in accordance with the procedures specified in this Article 00, which shall be the sole and exclusive procedures for the resolution of any such disputes.

## NEGOTIATION CLAUSES

## NEGOTIATION BETWEEN EXECUTIVES

*The parties shall attempt in good faith to resolve any dispute arising out of or relating to this Agreement promptly by negotiation between executives who have authority to settle the controversy and who are at a higher level of management than the persons with direct responsibility for administration of this contract. Any party may give the other party written notice of any dispute not resolved in the normal course of business. Within [15] days after delivery of the notice, the receiving party shall submit to the other a written response. The notice and the response shall include (a) a statement of each party's position and a summary of arguments supporting that position, and (b) the name and title of the executive who will represent that party and of any other person who will accompany the executive. Within [30] days after delivery of the disputing party's notice, the executives of both parties shall meet at a mutually acceptable time and place, and thereafter as often as they reasonably deem necessary, to attempt to resolve the dispute. All reasonable requests for information made by one party to the other will be honored.*

*All negotiations pursuant to this clause are confidential and shall be treated as compromise and settlement negotiations for purposes of applicable rules of evidence.*

### Commentary

Negotiation is, of course, the time-honored initial step in attempting to resolve disputes. However, because it can be difficult for the representatives of the parties who are directly involved in a dispute to resolve it, this clause requires, in the event of impasse between the initial negotiators, that the dispute be referred to senior executives of the parties whose presumably greater objectivity may make a successful resolution more likely.

## STEP NEGOTIATIONS (OPTION)

*If the matter has not been resolved by these persons within [45] days of the disputing party's notice, the dispute shall be referred to more senior executives of both parties who have authority to settle the dispute and who shall likewise meet to attempt to resolve the dispute.*

### Commentary

A variant of the ongoing negotiation procedure is the "step negotiation" technique under which the intermediate executives to whom the dispute has been referred will be required, if they are unsuccessful in resolving the problem, to refer the problem to more senior executives. A step negotiation clause would add the above provision to the "Negotiation Between Executives" clause, above.

# MEDIATION CLAUSES

## MEDIATION

If the dispute has not been resolved by negotiation within [45] days of the disputing party's notice, or if the parties failed to meet within [20] days, the parties shall endeavor to settle the dispute by mediation under the [then current] CPR Mediation Procedure [in effect on the date of this agreement]. Unless otherwise agreed, the parties will select a mediator from the CPR Panels of Distinguished Neutrals.

## MEDIATION WITH DESIGNATED NEUTRAL (OPTION)

If the dispute has not been resolved by negotiation within [45] days of the disputing party's notice, or if the parties failed to meet within [20] days, the parties shall endeavor to settle the dispute by mediation under the [then current] CPR Mediation Procedure [in effect on the date of this agreement]. The parties have selected _____ as the mediator in any such dispute, and [he] [she] has agreed to serve in that capacity and to be available on reasonable notice. In the event that _____ becomes unwilling or unable to serve, the parties have selected _____ as the alternative mediator. In the event that neither _____ nor _____ is willing or able to serve, the parties will agree on a substitute with the assistance of CPR. Unless otherwise agreed, the parties will select a mediator from the CPR Panels of Distinguished Neutrals.

### Commentary

It is often easier to agree on a neutral (or on the process for selecting a neutral) before any dispute actually arises. The neutral can be available for swift assistance if his or her selection and terms of retention have already been established.

# ARBITRATION CLAUSE

*Any dispute arising out of or relating to this contract or the breach, termination or validity thereof [which has not been resolved by a non-binding procedure as provided herein within [90] days of the initiation of such procedure,] shall be settled by arbitration in accordance with the [then current] CPR Rules for Non-Administered Arbitration [in effect on the date of this agreement,] by [a sole arbitrator] [three independent and impartial arbitrators, of whom each party shall appoint one], [three independent and impartial arbitrators, none of whom shall be appointed by either party]; [provided, however, that if either party will not participate in a non-binding procedure, the other may initiate arbitration before expiration of the above period]. The arbitration shall be governed by the Federal Arbitration Act, 9 U.S.C. §§ 1-16 to the exclusion of state laws inconsistent therewith, and judgment upon the award rendered by the arbitrator(s) may be entered by any court having jurisdiction thereof. The place of arbitration shall be _____. The arbitrator(s) [are] [are not] empowered to award damages in excess of compensatory damages [and each party hereby irrevocably waives any right to recover such damages with respect to any dispute resolved by arbitration].*

*The statute of limitations of the State of _____ applicable to the commencement of a lawsuit shall apply to the commencement of an arbitration hereunder, except that no defenses shall be available based upon the passage of time during any negotiation or mediation called for by the preceding paragraphs of this Article 00.*

*- or —*

# LITIGATION CLAUSE

*If the dispute has not been resolved by non-binding means as provided herein within 90 days of the initiation of such procedure, either party may initiate litigation [upon 00 days written notice to the other party]; provided, however, that if one party has requested the other to participate in a non-binding procedure and the other has failed to participate, the requesting party may initiate litigation before expiration of the above period.*

### Commentary

If non-binding procedures are unsuccessful and if the parties have not agreed on a binding ADR procedure, presumably they may go to court.

# ABBREVIATED CLAUSES
# FOR STANDARD BUSINESS AGREEMENTS

Abbreviated Clauses. The following short-form clauses that reflect the recommended multistep ADR scheme can be used in standard business agreements or in spot transactions such as purchase order forms. Mediation, with arbitration if necessary, is a multi-step process.

Optional clauses to protect rights during ADR appear below.

## NEGOTIATION CLAUSE

*The parties shall attempt in good faith to resolve any dispute arising out of or relating to this Agreement promptly by negotiation between executives.*

## MEDIATION CLAUSE

*The parties shall endeavor to resolve any dispute arising out of or relating to this Agreement by mediation under the CPR Mediation Procedure. Unless otherwise agreed, the parties will select a mediator from the CPR Panels of Distinguished Neutrals.*

# MEDIATION, WITH ARBITRATION IF NECESSARY

*The parties shall endeavor to resolve any dispute arising out of or relating to this agreement by mediation under the CPR Mediation Procedure. Unless the parties agree otherwise, the mediator will be selected from the CPR Panels of Distinguished Neutrals. Any controversy or claim arising out of or relating to this contract or the breach, termination or validity thereof, which remains unresolved 45 days after appointment of a mediator, shall be settled by arbitration by [a sole] [three] arbitrator(s) in accordance with the CPR Rules for Non-Administered Arbitration, and judgment upon the award rendered by the arbitrator(s) may be entered by any court having jurisdiction thereof.*

# ARBITRATION CLAUSE

*Any controversy or claim arising out of or relating to this contract or the breach, termination or validity thereof, shall be settled by arbitration by [a sole] [three] arbitrator(s) in accordance with the CPR Rules for Non-Administered Arbitration, and judgment upon the award rendered by the arbitrator(s) may be entered by any court having jurisdiction thereof.*

# OPTIONAL CLAUSES TO PROTECT RIGHTS

*Concerns sometimes arise that one party will try to avoid the agreed ADR procedure and win a "race to the courthouse." Consider a clause to "back-stop" ADR with an action to protect venue or for provisional relief to maintain the status quo pending ADR resolution. Clauses below also address needs to toll a statute of limitations or to continue performance pending ADR use.*

# PROVISIONAL REMEDIES

*The procedures specified in this Article 00 shall be the sole and exclusive procedures for the resolution of disputes between the parties arising out of or relating to this agreement; provided, however, that a party may file a complaint [for statute of limitations or venue reasons,] [to seek a preliminary injunction or other provisional judicial relief,] if in its sole judgment such action is necessary. Despite such action the parties will continue to participate in good faith in the procedures specified in this Article 00.*

## OPTION

*If the agreement of the parties to use ADR breaks down and a later application for an injunction is made, the parties will not assert a defense of laches or statute of limitation, based upon the time spent on ADR.*

## TOLLING STATUTE OF LIMITATIONS

*All applicable statutes of limitation and defenses based upon the passage of time shall be tolled while the procedures specified in this Article 00 are pending. The parties will take such action, if any, required to effectuate such tolling.*

## PERFORMANCE TO CONTINUE

*Each party is required to continue to perform its obligations under this contract pending final resolution of any dispute arising out of or relating to this contract [unless to do so would be impossible or impracticable under the circumstances].*

## RIGHT OF TERMINATION

*The requirements of this Article 00 shall not be deemed a waiver of any right of termination under this contract.*

# LEGAL CONCERNS

## ENFORCEABILITY

*Properly drafted arbitration agreements generally are specifically enforceable in U.S. courts and in the courts of many other industrial nations. Although several lower courts have enforced agreements to mediate future disputes (see AMF Inc. v. Brunswick Corp., 621 F. Supp. 456 (E.D. NY 1985), it is not certain that agreements to negotiate or conduct a non-binding ADR proceeding will be specifically enforced by the court. Moreover, the CPR Mediation Procedure permits either party to withdraw. Nevertheless, agreements to use mediation between responsible companies should carry considerable weight and, experience shows, will substantially increase the likelihood of a consensual resolution.*

## CONFIDENTIALITY

Maintaining the confidentiality of information disclosed and positions taken in the course of dispute settlement negotiations, mediation or arbitration procedures is a common concern. The CPR procedures, referred to in these rules, provide contractual assurance of confidentiality, at Rule 17 in the CPR Rules for Non-Administered Arbitration and at Section 9 in the CPR Mediation Procedure. In addition, mediation proceedings are facilitated settlement negotiations and as such are entitled to the protection accorded by Rule 408 of the Federal Rules of Evidence and state counterparts. The legislatures of more than 40 states have enacted statutes broadening that protection for mediation.

## DISCOVERY IN ADR

One benefit of ADR is that the costly, burdensome and time-consuming discovery that typifies much litigation can be avoided. ADR procedures can incorporate streamlined discovery to enable the parties to assess their respective positions. The informal exchange of relevant documents and information is common in both binding and non-binding ADR. The neutral or

ADR tribunal can play an important role in facilitating discovery. Depositions of key witnesses may occur in the preparatory phase of arbitrations under Rule 10 of the CPR Rules for Non-Administered Arbitration which states that "The Tribunal shall permit and facilitate such discovery as it shall determine is appropriate in the circumstance...." Under the CPR Mediation Procedure, at Section 4, parties can jointly consult with the mediator to establish a discovery schedule. Absent agreement to do discovery, however, it may not be compelled in a non-binding process.

# ARBITRATION COMMENTARY

***Characteristics of Arbitration.*** Virtually any issue regarding arbitration procedure may be addressed by agreement. Far from being monolithic, arbitration can be what the parties make it. Selection of a well qualified arbitrator or panel possessing managerial skills and determined to expedite the proceeding is perhaps the single most important factor in assuring a proceeding that is both fair and efficient.

***One Arbitrator or Three?*** The proceeding is likely to be significantly more expeditious and economical if the parties select one arbitrator rather than three. Nevertheless, in large cases some parties may have greater confidence in a panel of three arbitrators. Under the CPR Rules, party-appointed arbitrators are required to be independent and impartial. Nevertheless, CPR discourages the use of party-appointed arbitrators.

***Arbitrator Selection.*** The CPR Rules give the parties ample opportunity to select a tribunal on their own. If they fail, however, either party may request CPR assistance in the manner specified in Rule 6.

***Arbitrate All or Certain Disputes?*** Some attorneys favor provisions that are limited to certain kinds of disputes or disputes involving less than a stipulated sum; however, such limitations may give rise to arbitrability defenses and thus breed litigation. They should therefore be used with caution.

***Place of Arbitration.*** It is desirable to designate the place of arbitration in the arbitration clause, recognizing that the place can be changed thereafter by mutual agreement. Rule 9.6 of the CPR Rules empowers the Tribunal to fix the place of arbitration absent agreement by the parties.

***Punitive Damages.*** The availability of punitive damages in arbitration may rest on the parties' express agreement. If the parties wish to preclude the arbitrator(s) from awarding punitive damages or other damages in excess of compensatory damages, the arbitration agreement should state that the arbitrator(s) are not empowered to award such damages and that the parties waive the right to recover such damages. Otherwise the arbitrator(s) may be able to award additional damages, or possibly a separate legal action may be brought seeking such additional damages. If the parties wish to permit an award of damages in excess of compensatory damages, they should so state. In *Mastrobuono v. Shearson-Lehman Hutton Inc.,* 115 S. Ct. 1213 (1995), the court found that a bar to the award of punitive damages did not arise simply from a statement that New York law applied to the contract. Case law in New York precludes awards of punitive damages by arbitrators.

***Pre-Award Interest.*** Under the CPR Rules the arbitrator(s) may award interest, including pre-award interest. However, if the parties wish to ensure that pre-award interest will be awarded, it is advisable to so state in the arbitration clause. It is also advisable to specify the method of computation of such interest.

***Written Opinions.*** Rule 13.2 of the CPR Rules provides that "All awards shall be in writing and shall state the reasoning on which the award rests unless the parties agree otherwise." If the parties prefer a "bare" award, they may so provide.

***Governing Law & Preemption.*** If the parties wish to have the law of a particular jurisdiction govern as to substantive matters, they should provide in their agreement that the law of that jurisdiction, inclusive or exclusive of its conflict-of-laws rules, shall govern as to the merits of the dispute.

The Federal Arbitration Act, 9 U.S.C. § 1-16 ("FAA"), governs arbitration agreements in contracts involving interstate or international commerce and supplies various rules for arbitration proceedings unless the parties specify otherwise. In *Volt Information Sciences, Inc. v. Board of Trustees of the Leland Stanford Junior University*, 489 U.S. 468 (1989), the Supreme Court held that the FAA did not preempt application of contrary provisions of state arbitration law. In *Volt*, the parties' agreement expressly incorporated the laws of California to govern the arbitration process. To ensure that the FAA will apply, regardless of the law which they have specified to govern on substantive issues, the arbitration clause should provide that the arbitration will be conducted under the FAA to the exclusion of state laws inconsistent therewith or which would produce a different result.

***Judicial Review of Arbitration Awards.*** The grounds for vacation of an arbitration award normally are limited to arbitrator misconduct, partiality, corruption and the like. (*See* Section 10 of the FAA and state counterparts.) Most parties opting for arbitration consider the finality of the award a major advantage. The rare arbitration agreement will provide for an appeal to an appellate arbitration tribunal. Agreements permitting court review also are not unknown, but the courts are divided on whether to accept such appeals.

***Statute of Limitations.*** Statutes of limitation typically relate to the commencement of actions in court and their application to an arbitration proceeding may well be at the discretion of the arbitrator. It is advisable, therefore, either to provide in the arbitration clause that the statute of limitations of a particular state will be deemed to apply or to establish a specific time limitation on the commencement of an arbitrated proceeding, e.g.:

> *Any claim by either party shall be time-barred unless the asserting party commences an arbitration proceeding with respect to such claim within one year after the basis for such claim [has arisen,] [became known to the asserting party,] [subject to paragraph 00 hereof relating to tolling of time limitations].*

***Arbitration Variations.*** Several variations of the basic arbitration concept have become popular. In "final offer" or "baseball" arbitration each party submits a final offer amount and the arbitrator or tribunal must make an award in either amount. In "bounded" or "high-low" arbitration the parties agree that the respondent will pay damages within a specified range and that an award outside that range will be modified accordingly. These variations can minimize each party's risk of exposure to an extreme award.

***Special Arbitration Rules.*** CPR has issued Rules for Non-Administered Arbitration of Patent and Trade Secret Disputes and an Employment Dispute Arbitration Procedure. If the agreement in question is between parties in different countries, the CPR International Arbitration Rules should be substituted.

***Clauses to Discourage Adjudication.*** One effective way of encouraging parties to resolve their dispute by non-adjudicative means and of discouraging litigation or arbitration is to include in the contract language empowering the judge or arbitrator to require the losing party to reimburse the prevailing party, wholly or in part, for legal fees and other expenses incurred by that party in the litigation or arbitration. A variation would be to limit reimbursement of the prevailing party to the amount of fees and expenses incurred by the losing party. The CPR Rules empower the arbitrators to apportion the costs of arbitration, including attorneys' fees, among the parties in such manner as the arbitrators deem reasonable. Another technique is to provide that if one party declines the other's best offer in non-binding ADR and initiates arbitration or litigation, the outcome of which is not significantly more favorable to that party, it shall pay the other party's cost of the arbitration or litigation.

# APPENDIX J

## THE HALLIBURTON DISPUTE RESOLUTION PROGRAM

Reprinted with permission of Halliburton, Inc.

## INTRODUCTION

The new Halliburton Dispute Resolution Program is a four-option plan for resolving problems that happen at work. It encourages open communication, protects your work relationships and helps keep costs and tempers under control. For serious legal disputes, it also makes available the experience and objectivity of the American Arbitration Association (AAA).

*Founded in 1926, the American Arbitration Association (AAA) helps businesses, associations, and all levels of government resolve over 60,000 cases each year.*

## FOUR OPTIONS—AN OVERVIEW

***Option One—The Open Door Policy*** helps you solve your problem early through the ***Chain of Command***. Discuss it with your Business Unit Personnel or Corporate Employee Relations. An ***Employee Hotline***, (800) (telephone number), puts you in touch with a confidential Adviser who can also help you. If you think your problem is serious enough, you may want to request a ***Legal Consultation***. If approved, Halliburton will pay for most of it.

***Option Two—The Conference*** is the next step if your problem is still unresolved. You can sit down with a Company representative and the Program Administrator to decide what process you would like to use to settle your dispute. If both parties agree, an in-house resolution process can be arranged. If your dispute involves a legally protected right, such as protection from discrimination or harassment, you may prefer to go to mediation or arbitration through AAA.

*Option Three—Mediation* lets you and the Company discuss your legal dispute with a neutral third party, AAA. The neutral party or mediator can listen to both sides of the story and help you work it out together. To use AAA, you pay a processing fee of $50. ***Mediation is only for disputes involving legally protected rights.***

*Option Four—Arbitration* lets you present your legal dispute to a neutral third party, AAA, for a final decision. The arbitrator will decide your case after hearing arguments from both sides. AAA can make an award just like a judge in the court system. To use AAA, you pay a fee of $50, unless you have already paid it for mediation. ***Arbitration is only for disputes involving legally protected rights.***

## QUESTIONS AND ANSWERS

1.  **How does the new Open Door Policy differ from the old one?**

    For the first time in the history of the Company, the Open Door Policy has been put into writing. Both old and new Open Door Policies call for resolving workplace disputes through the Chain of Command. Improvements to the Policy include an Employee Hotline, the opportunity to talk with an Adviser and if approved, a legal consultation for serious, legal disputes. Halliburton will be training all of its managers and supervisors how to use the new program.

2. **What do I do if the supervisor I approach ignores the Open Door Policy?**

If the first person you approach under the Open Door Policy doesn't help you, proceed immediately to another level of supervision in the Chain of Command. You may also want to call the Employee Hotline at (800) (telephone number) or call your Business Unit Personnel Manager or Employee Relations.

3. **What happens if my supervisor starts to make things difficult for me after I complain?**

Take your problem to a higher level in the Chain of Command, or to an Advisor through the Employee Hotline. The Advisor will help you decide on a strategy for handling your problem or refer you to someone in the Chain of Command.

4. **Can I use the Halliburton Dispute Resolution Program to solve any problem that happens at work?**

You may use Options One, **the Open Door Policy**, and Two, **the Conference**, to address any workplace dispute.

Options Three and Four, the AAA processes, can be used to resolve only those problems or disputes involving legally protected rights, such as: discrimination for age, sex or religion, on-the job harassment, or being asked to commit unlawful acts.

5. **How does arbitration differ from a court trial?**

With arbitration, the decision is final; except under rare circumstances, it may not be reversed by subsequent proceedings. With a trial court decision, an appeal may be filed causing endless delays. Also, an arbitration proceeding is usually much more informal than a case in court. The biggest difference, however, lies in the reasonable cost of arbitration. Because arbitration is faster and less formal, it ends up costing much less to prepare the case for both the employee and employer.

6.    **If I don't like the arbitrator's decision, can I appeal it through the court system?**

Arbitration awards are final, binding and may be enforced under the law, with only limited appeals allowed through the courts.

**EMPLOYEE HOTLINE**
**CALL (800) (telephone number)**

Effective January 1, 1998, Halliburton will adopt this four-option program as the exclusive means of resolving workplace disputes for legally protected rights. That means if you accept or continue your job at Halliburton after that date, you will agree to resolve all legal claims against Halliburton through this process instead of through the court system.

# APPENDIX K

## NEGOTIATION PLAN FOR DISPUTE RESOLUTION IN LITIGATION

This "Negotiating Plan" was prepared by Carrie Menkel-Meadow, Professor of Law and Director, Georgetown-Hewlett Program in Conflict Resolution and Legal Problem Solving, Georgetown University Law Center, copyright 1980. Permission granted.

I.    **Needs And Interests**

    A.    Client's Needs

        1. Now known:

            a. Legal
            b. Economic
            c. Social
            d. Psychological
            e. Risk Aversion
            f.  Political/moral/ethical/religious
            g. Other

        2. To be discovered (interview subjects):

    B.    Other Party's Needs

        1. Now known

            a. Legal
            b. Economic
            c. Social
            d. Psychological

      e. Risk Aversion
      f. Political/moral/ethical/religious
      g. Other

   2. To be discovered (questions to be pursued in discovery, negotiation):

C.    Consequences/Outcomes of Trial/Settlement

   1. Client

      a. Trial

         1) if wins, what
         2) if loses, what

      b. Settlement — consequences:

   2. Other Party

      a. Trial

         1) if wins, what
         2) if loses, what

   3. BATNA (Best Alternative to Negotiated Settlement)

      a. client
      b. other party

## II.   Legal Merits and Litigation Risk Analysis

A.    What are the legal issues to be resolved in this dispute?

(legal liabilities and remedial issues)

B.  Outline the principal arguments for each of the foregoing issues that suggest your client will prevail.  For each argument, identify the following:

.

1. The applicable legal principle (legal authority) supporting the argument, and;

2. Each element of that legal principle that will have to be proven with a statement of

>   a. The evidence establishing that element and its source (i.e. witness or document);
>   b. The admissibility of the evidence; and
>   c. The credibility or persuasiveness of that evidence.

C.  Outline the principal arguments on each of the foregoing issues that suggest that the other side will prevail.  For each argument identify:

1. The applicable legal authority (to support the argument)

2. Each element of that legal principle, specifying source (witness or document):

>   a.  The evidence establishing that element and its source (i.e. witness or document);
>   b.  The admissibility of the evidence; and
>   c.  The credibility or persuasiveness of that evidence.

D.  What factors are likely to affect the parties willingness to proceed with the litigation (social, psychological, etc.):

1. Client
2. Other Party

E.    Evaluate the likelihood of success on each of the claims listed above. (Who is likely to prevail and why?  You may use predictive language expressed as probabilities if those can be justified).

F.    Economic Value of each party's legal claims'

1. Client
2. Other Party

G.    Assessment of probabilities for prevailing (combining legal, risk aversion, economic and other factors) (express as probabilities of legal recoveries) :

1. Client
2. Other Party

## III.   Proposals, Solutions, and Principled Negotiation: Substantive Strategies

A.    What is at stake in the dispute? (Underlying needs and interests of the parties)

1. What
2. Who is involved?
3. When
4. Where
5. How

B.    What needs/interests are shared by the parties?

C.    What needs/interests are different for the parties?

D.    What solutions are suggested by the above?  (Meeting the needs/interest of both sides; what Pareto optimal solutions are suggested by the needs, facts, and consequences of legal action; contrast court-ordered legal remedies to others that might be available.) List possibilities here (multiple proposals).

E. For each potential solution identified in paragraph D above, list the arguments or principles which support your proposed solution, taking account of the evaluation of the legal merits and the parties' underlying needs and interests.

## IV. Negotiation Strategy

A. What information is needed from other side (needs, interest, factual information, assessment of case, etc.). How will this information be obtained? (Specify questions to be asked, discovery plans, etc.)

B. What information is likely to be sought from you? How will you respond (and why)?

C. Agenda (what subjects or issues should be addressed in order to resolve the dispute? What preference do you have about order?)

D. Planning, articulating, and scripting principled reasons. For each proposal listed above, specify the reason for that proposal and the likely response from other side:

*Proposal #1:*

Principled Reason:

Other Party Response:

*Proposal #2:*

Principled Reason:

Other Party Response:

*Proposal #3:*

Principled Reason:

Other Party Response:

E.     Proposals Anticipated from the Other Side

Responses:

Note:     Appropriate use of this plan should include sufficient space to provide for multiple and reflective responses to each item.

5

# APPENDIX L
## ADR WEBSITES
## INTERNET RESOURCES FOR DISPUTE RESOLUTION

### Selecting a Mediator

American Arbitration Association
www.adr.org

American College of Civil Trial Mediators
www.acctm.org

CPR Institute for Dispute Resolution
www.cpradr.org

International Academy of Mediators
www.iamed.org

JAMS The Resolution Experts
www.jamsadr.com

World Intellectual Property Organization
Arbitration and Mediation Center
www.arbiter.wipo.int

### U.S. Government

U.S. Department of Justice – Office of
Dispute Resolution
www.usdoj.gov/odr

### Labor

U.S. Department of Labor
www.dol.gov

National Labor Relations Board
www.nlrb.gov

### Construction

Associated General Contractors
www.agc.org
National Association of Home Builders
www.nahb.com

### Employment

Center for Employment Dispute
Resolution
www.cedr-adr-consortium.org

Equal Employment Advisory Council
www.eeac.org

### Healthcare

American Health Lawyers Association
Alternative Dispute Resolution Service
www.healthlawyers.com

## Current Development/Issues

ADR World.com
  www.adrworld.com

American Bar Association Section of
Dispute Resolution
  www.abanet.org/dispute

Mediate.com
  www.mediate.com

## International

American Arbitration Association
  www.adr.org

Centre for Effective Dispute Resolution
  www.cedr.co.uk

International Chamber of Commerce
  www.iccwbo.org

London Court of International Arbitration
  www.lcia-arbitration.com/lcia

World Intellectual Property Organization
Arbitration and Mediation Center
  www.arbiter.wipo.int

# INDEX